Praise for *The NIC*

"Whether you're driven by necessity or oppor offers the perfect combination of information on the path to entrepreneurial success. Penina out of business startup. Follow her simple formula: Creativity + Passion + Timing = Entrepreneurial Success and you'll unlock the secrets of achieving your dreams of business ownership."

— **RIEVA LESONSKY,** Founder/CEO of GrowBiz Media

"Penina Rybak is a passionate, thoughtful advocate for women's entrepreneurship. She has a deep understanding of the tools, resources and models which will help women to launch viable businesses, which is critical to the future success of our economy."

— **PAMELA SLIM,** business coach and bestselling author of *Body of Work* and *Escape from Cubicle Nation*

"I enjoyed reading the book and got great ideas from it! Penina's writing is beautiful and inspirational! She not only tells us how to be successful but how to make the world a better place while feeling complete as a person. Her insightful knowledge of social media and new technology is both refreshing and energizing. I love the way she encourages us to think outside the box and grow. She also uses history and current culture to teach us how to best serve our community and relate in a "NICE" humanitarian way. This is an entertaining read peppered with movie reviews and words of wisdom."

— **ERIN WILSON,** Founder, QRCode ID

"*The NICE Reboot* does a great job of motivating and mentoring a large and growing group of entrepreneurs — women! I do believe that women have the edge, with their high emotional IQ, to create the "new business culture" that every worker wants — better role definitions, more effective and productive leadership, and better work-life balance. I like Penina's idea of convincing them to reboot, if necessary, to achieve that potential."

— **MARTY ZWILLING,** Founder & CEO of Startup Professionals, Inc.

"*The NICE Reboot* provides LOTS of information for the wannabe entrepreneur."

— **GERI STENGEL,** President of Ventureneer and Stengel Solutions

The NICE
Reboot

HOW TO BALANCE YOUR CRAVINGS
FOR HUMANITY AND TECHNOLOGY
IN TODAY'S STARTUP CULTURE

The NICE Reboot

A Guide to Becoming a Better Female Entrepreneur

Penina Rybak

MAVEN HOUSE
PRESS

Published by Maven House Press, 4 Snead Ct., Palmyra, VA 22963; 610.883.7988; www.mavenhousepress.com.

Special discounts on bulk quantities of Maven House Press books are available to corporations, professional associations, and other organizations. For details contact the publisher.

For information about subsidiary rights (translation, audio, book club, serial, etc.) contact rights@mavenhousepress.com.

While this publication is designed to provide accurate and authoritative information in regard to the subject matter covered, it is sold with the understanding that the publisher is not engaged in rendering legal, accounting, or other professional service. If legal advice or other expert assistance is required, the services of a competent professional person should be sought. — From the Declaration of Principles jointly adopted by a Committee of the American Bar Association and a Committee of Publishers and Associations

This book is an independent publication and has not been authorized, sponsored, or otherwise approved by any of the companies mentioned in the book.

Library of Congress Control Number: 2013958093

Paperback ISBN: 978-1-938548-18-5
ePUB ISBN: 978-1-938548-19-2
ePDF ISBN: 978-1-938548-20-8

Printed in the United States of America.

10 9 8 7 6 5 4 3 2 1

CONTENTS

Contents

PENINA'S POINTERS

LIST OF FIGURES

ACKNOWLEDGMENTS

The best books come from someplace inside. You don't write because you want to, but because you have to.

— Judy Blume

Think like a wise man but communicate in the language of the people.

— William Butler Yeats

I WOULD LIKE TO THANK the following people and organizations who have either physically or spiritually accompanied me and knowingly or unknowingly mentored me and inspired me to choose the converging paths of an entrepreneur, writer, and iPad evangelist.

I need to first acknowledge my immeasurable thanks and humble appreciation to God for the experiences, traits, and gifts I've been given, which have helped me navigate my meandering journey to this point. I must acknowledge how much my friends and "my kids"— my pediatric clients and students — have taught me over the years. How you all have enriched my life for having known you, even if it was sometimes for a short period of time. Kudos to my family, my immediate one, and the Hochstein one, my second one, for their support and encouragement to write this book. I want to express my heartfelt gratitude to the entire staff at the Apple Store in Paramus, New Jersey, especially Christa Hughes, Rob Pollack, and the rest of my IT team — Jose YBarra, Keith Mandeville, Vlad Grosu, Mike McLaughlin, and Danielle Scott — for their ongoing roles as teachers and rainmakers for so many people, including me. You are all awesome role models of what it means to be generous with your time and knowledge. Especially Morah Hochstein at the New York Store. You guys rock!

I want to sincerely thank Dr. Susan Fralick-Ball, Penny Graham, Zita Moses, Anne Winters, Tony Gross, and my editor Jim Pennypacker for their support, continued faith in me and my mission, and reading and contributing to my paper trail. I appreciate all our talks and correspondence. I also want to say kudos to my lovely librarians Alice Weisser and Veronica Olshefski and the rest of the staff at the Maurice Pine Public Library in Fair Lawn, New Jersey, for their unflagging cheer, courtesy, and camaraderie. You are all such a credit to your institution.

Finally, I want to thank Erma Bombeck, Steve Jobs, Guy Kawasaki, Seth Godin, Evan Burfield, Rieva Lesonsky, Pamela Slim, Diane Bertolin, Martin Zwilling, James Altucher, Joss Whedon, Tim Kring, Shel Silverstein, and Betty MacDonald (author of the beloved children's books, *The Mrs. Piggle Wiggle Series*) for the profound effects your thinking and writings have had on my behaviors and on the growth of my theory of mind.

I'm a better person and certainly a much better entrepreneur than I would have been had I not been introduced to all your voices and ideas at pivotal moments in my life. Patterns. Seemingly random events but actually part of a pattern. The strides I've made both personally and professionally through my exposure to all of you have coalesced into one entity — this book. Finally, I salute female entrepreneurs everywhere for reading this book and for all the endeavors you engage in. I'd love to know what else I can do to help. We're all in this together. Be in touch. Cheers!

— Penina Rybak

PREFACE

Cinder-Nechah to the rescue.... Let's do this!

— Dr. Nechah Hochstein, 1971–2012

An idea is a feat of association.

— Robert Frost

THIS BOOK IS DEDICATED to the memory of my best friend, first and most treasured mentor, Apple Techie and fellow Mac Girl from way back when, Trekkie pal, Buffy buddy, and all around hero, Dr. Natalie "Nechah" Hochstein, Psy.D. She was a true scholar, lady, and a brilliant analyst of human behavior. She effortlessly and elegantly taught me so much, from the time I met her in late childhood until she lost her valiant battle to breast cancer in December 2012. Most of all, she taught me to work hard, think like a child, laugh often, and readily share information with others in need. She was my sister in arms, my cheerleader, and my muse. She is sorely missed, but echoes of her vast wisdom live on — on a daily basis in my work and actions and in the words found on these pages. Any misinformation or poor word choices are my fault alone. I humbly ask for the reader's understanding.

People, women in particular, often ask me what started me on this road of self-employment, of becoming a startup entrepreneur in 2010 in the middle of a terrible recession. What made me change course after being a school-based, pediatric speech therapist, autism specialist, and educational technology consultant for two decades? Although I was part of a wonderfully collaborative team process and a unique group of employees (and accruing steady vacation days, water cooler conversations, and medical and retirement benefits), I realized that I wanted more. I enjoyed working in the school system but nonetheless felt that something was missing. What gave me that self-realization that resulted in a clarity of vision causing me to alter the trajectory of my career?

Unlike a single epiphany, my eureka moment was a necklace of several sequential events. My realizations were like a burst of fireworks, consecutively and dramatically suspended in midair, glaringly obvious for me to see and analyze. They began in 2005 when I finally extricated myself from a failed marriage. This first one started exactly a month before 9/11 and, like 9/11, left heartache, devastation, and disillusionment in its wake. Now I had to learn to rely on myself and enjoy my own company again. I had to start over. Learn a whole new set of rules. Make up a few of my own. So I did.

I climbed out of the box — the one people were so eagerly trying to stuff me into — to make sense of me, to help me make sense of myself. To quote Deepak Chopra, "Instead of thinking outside the box, get rid of the box!" I decided to relinquish fear of the unknown, of failure, and to embrace change. To lower the volume of the voices around me and concentrate on heeding my own inner voice, which had gotten steadily softer over time.

I actively redesigned my inner landscape, which resulted in changing my outer one. My behaviors. My outlooks. My approaches to how I related to the world around me. How I related to my young students with autism and special needs who I had so desperately been trying to reach for years as both a speech therapist and a human being. It worked. For a while. Until the rules changed again.

In the late winter of 2008, with no warning, my appendix ruptured and I almost died. I remember thinking I had food poisoning, but when I started to vomit blood, I realized that I would have to brave a snowy Northeastern Saturday night and drive myself to the hospital. I still took time to pack a suitcase with pajamas, toiletries, and a mini DVD player to watch Joss Whedon's accolade to female empowerment — Buffy Summers — in action. Even then I wanted to be prepared and empowered and stave off boredom in case I had to wait for hours. I did. It was a long night. The doctors got to me in time, barely. There were complications post-surgery, which happened hours after I checked into the emergency room. I spent extra time in the hospital and weeks at home recuperating. Needless to say, my perceptions about my reality and my purpose in life began to shift. I had to throw out the playbook and start over once more. So I did. Back to the drawing board. Life went on, a bit differently from before, but smooth sailing again, sort of.

In the late summer of 2009, my best friend and mentor, Dr. Nechah Hochstein, was diagnosed with stage IV breast cancer. Life as I knew it, which had been rebooted twice already, now halted and stayed that way for a while. At least it felt like it did. I felt lost and frozen inside, like the spinning ball of doom, which I'm sure fellow Mac users know about and loathe the way I do. My own inner landscape had seismic activity and was forever transformed. The ensuing months of dawning realization that life really is short and rather unfair, coupled with the sobering reality of helping and watching Nechah go through the ups and downs of painful surgery and prolonged chemotherapy, had a profound effect on my own perspective, my theory of mind.

I once again had to reevaluate my life, my career, my relationships, and my acceptance of the status quo. The status quo accepted by many women in the workplace, just trying to survive. The status quo Nechah had no choice about living with, as deteriorating health made her downsize her dreams of opening her own private practice in New York City. She taught me a lot about determination and perseverance that last year of her life. She actually did it. She managed to rent office space, in downtown New York City no less, and get many clients. She assisted quite a surprising number of people that last year, paid and pro-bono, whom I only learned of after her passing.

Nechah started her own business while joking that she was treading water. Like many women, I too had felt that I spent the day at work treading water. How many times have you felt like you were in a churning ocean of ever-changing tides? I started to rethink things, including the idea that, although I might not be able to redirect these tides, I might do something to alter the volume of the ebb and flow.

So I began to swim against the tide and look for new land. My land. The one I think about when I picture a nicer, more humane society, a more equal workplace, and a more innovative female entrepreneur, one who leaves her mark. A physical and psychic mark, a legacy, the way Nechah did, that will last long after she's gone.

I have a confession to make. I'm a big fan of using pop culture references to make my point. My friends know this. My seminar audiences have learned this. Now you will too. Nechah and I were fascinated by two recent critically acclaimed TV shows — one that captured the mainstream television viewer's interest, *Lost,* and one that captured ours, *Touch.* We were impressed with the premises and themes of both shows and discussed them often. They focused on different characters and settings, yet there were common threads that we found interesting, both as educators and startup entrepreneurs.

I started watching *Touch* because of rumors that it featured a nonverbal boy with autism. I stayed for the extra helping of existential, beautifully scaffolded story lines. I initially started watching *Lost* because of the tantalizing premise of people starting over. I stayed for the extra helping of nail-biting suspense and self-realizations that the characters experienced.

Nechah and I spent countless hours analyzing these two TV shows for thinkers — the implications and lessons learned from visiting the shows' universes and the repeating themes. The first was the theme of patterns. Tim Kring, visionary creator of *Touch* (and *Heroes,* which we also loved watching and dissecting), is a masterful story teller. He is definitely as curious about the concept of interconnectivity as we were (we called it patterns).

My maternal grandmother used to love sewing, needlepoint in particular. As a little girl I was always amazed as I watched her work. I couldn't get over how one side of her tapestry was a mess, a jumble of discordance. There were threads everywhere, no emerging likeness of anything I could identify. But the other side of the tapestry, the side she was working on, slowly revealed the picture she had in mind — a butterfly, a field of flowers, a home on a lake. Nechah and I frequently pondered the meaning of life's tapestry and the idea behind the butterfly effect—the idea that a small event (a butterfly moving its wings) could possibly affect a significant event (altering the path of a tornado). We talked about the importance of knowledge and observation. We tried to make sense of seemingly disparate patterns that form over time. We wanted to understand how people's behavior results from collective experiences and how skewed perceptions of those experiences can then interrupt their path.

This book is about sharing the emerging patterns of entrepreneurship I've learned, from Nechah, from my own experiences, and from others. People whose paths have intersected with mine, deliberately or seemingly randomly (I believe that nothing is random). I believe that patterns are everything. Patterns shape behavior and perceptions. Patterns can be found everywhere, especially in entrepreneurship.

The second common thread we both found interesting about the two TV shows I mentioned was the concept of interpersonal and intrapersonal growth through forging connections with others. Forging connections to help implement steps toward personal emancipation and redemption. Freedom. From previous thought patterns. From past experiences and deeds. From obsolete best practices, both in education and in business. By using your own behavior — reactions to surrounding events — coupled with technology to effect positive change. To redirect the tides of change in both the trajectory and outcome of a new plan.

My maternal grandfather, who was another crucial mentor and important person in my life, unexpectedly passed away soon after Nechah. He had followed my unfolding entrepreneurship and travels. We had been having regular phone calls for years, debating the merits of using technology to spur personal growth, both spiritually and financially, right until he got sick and passed.

Both *Touch* and *Lost,* interestingly, highlighted our increasing collective dependence on technology, for better or for worse. They showcased the characters' personal struggles to harness it or to overcome the physical, mental, and emotional obstacles created by it. Nechah and I frequently discussed the idea of a personal credo one should live by. We also discussed the contradictory outcomes of technology, as an agent of inclusion that shrinks the global community and an agent of fragmentation that segments humanity. We talked about the cyber-bullying and antisocial behaviors that were on the rise, as younger and younger children get indoctrinated into the *Hunger Games* paradigm being played out in society today. We pondered technology's strengths and weaknesses, as both a positively and negatively disruptive element in world markets, entrepreneurship, and education. We debated future outcomes in these areas that result from constant multisensory rivers of information that flow through the Internet and society's increasing appetite and reliance on tech inventions to fish from it.

There's a saying, "Give a man a fish and he eats for a day. Teach the man to fish and he eats for life." In other words, it's better to show you how to do something than to do it for you. This book is meant to do just that. Written from the perspective of a child-centric behaviorist, as Nechah used to call me, the book is about giving female entrepreneurs (you) a behavioral blueprint and practical tools for your toolbox for fishing in the waters of your choice. It's about harnessing your nurturing psyche and proficiency with technology and balancing the two. It's about synthesizing your innate and learned skills to help facilitate your own personal emancipation from outdated arenas and fear of the unknown and start you on your own endeavor to grow, change, and soar.

"Join the Journey for Change" has been my company's motto since I launched Socially Speaking™ LLC in 2010. I invite you to join the journey too. Welcome to my new inner landscape, which has influenced my philosophy and journey as an entrepreneur. It has shaped my ideas and approach, which I have dubbed The NICE Reboot, and an offshoot, The NICE Initiative. This is my entrepreneurial footprint for others to see and maybe follow initially before forging their own path and embarking on their own journey for change. Change is scary. Change is hard. But change is good. Change will nourish your soul and set your creativity free. Change will reshape the world, one person and deed at a time. It's time.

INTRODUCTION

The most difficult thing is the decision to act, the rest is mere tenacity. You can do anything you decide to do. You can act to change and control your life; and the procedure, the process, is its own reward.

— Amelia Earhart

Every generation needs a revolution.

— Thomas Jefferson

SOME PEOPLE CLAIM that women, more so than men, tend to multitask more often in their personal lives. Yet this multitasking somehow yields less overall job satisfaction, less overall assertiveness, and less achievement of goals in their professional lives. Is this true today? And if so, who's to blame: biology, society, lack of education? I think all three factors have contributed somewhat to this phenomenon. Although there's an underground movement afoot named the

Entrepreneurial Revolution, an offshoot of the *Tech Revolution,* more and more women are still taken by surprise when they're asked to join one or both. Why is that? Don't today's women have the pioneering spirit to "boldly go where no one has gone before," as they say in the Star Trek universe? Don't today's women value innovation, creativity, and individuality and strive to achieve all three?

Here's another sticky question: Are we collectively prepared for the new revolutions? Despite the plethora of information available over the Internet, the continued reverence for the American Dream, and the increased college enrollment of female students, there is still doubt. There still seems to be a noticeable chasm between men and women when it comes to entrepreneurial readiness. The good news is that these new movements are not like the exclusive "boy's clubs" of yesteryear. Remember childhood power plays? Remember your brother attending an all boys' secret meeting in the garage, where the neighborhood girls were left out in the cold, literally, faces pressed up against the glass?

There are noticeably more female trailblazers now than in the past who are full members of both revolutions. They have already left their mark and paved the way for others to follow. These include women like Oprah Winfrey, with her book club and her TV network, OWN; Marissa Meyer, CEO at Yahoo; Sheryl Sandberg, COO of Facebook and bestselling author of *Lean In;* Arianna Huffington, editor-in-chief of *The Huffington Post;* Shari Arison, CEO of the Arison Group and bestselling author of *Activate Your Goodness;* Robin Chase, former founder and CEO of ZipCar; and Kathy Ireland, nicknamed in 2012 by *Forbes* magazine as the "Super Model Turned Super Mogul" for her international company, kiWW.

There's never been a better time for a female entrepreneur to come into her own. To carve a niche for herself. To promote change. Look at all the new websites, social media sites, and female empowerment blogs popping up, created by women, for women, who are just graduating college and beyond.

Yet despite creating thoughtful, well-crafted mission statements, exhibiting initiative and good time management, and understanding the power of collaboration, many women who become entrepreneurs will flounder and even fail. Many women today still seem to feel hesitant about upping their tech-savvy quotient and thinking outside the box. Women often feel that it's safer to play by the rules, many of which were certainly not written by us, for us, or even about us and who we really are!

In studies of young girls and boys, the research has shown that girls tend to display a higher emotional IQ. I've seen this in my experiences as a pediatric speech therapist, and many parents have reported this from their personal experience. A person's emotional quotient, or EQ, is what makes him or her empathetic, intuitive, collaborative, and, well, nice! Yet as we ladies mature, we get mixed signals about using these skills in our arsenal, especially in the workplace when performing, competing for raises and promotions, and negotiating to effect change or a different outcome during projects. These mixed signals result in diminished humanity, fragmented mentorship and courtesy, and cutthroat competitiveness, so often seen in today's workplaces.

I was raised to believe that courtesy is really a verb, not the noun that's defined in *The Merriam-Webster Dictionary* as "a behavior marked by respect for others." I learned as a child that courtesy partially involves the pursuit of knowledge and the sharing of that knowledge to help others. It's the highest form of human interaction and one's purpose in life. I internalized these lessons and used them when I became a pediatric speech-language pathologist and autism specialist, and again as an entrepreneur.

I clearly remember my orientation day in graduate school at New York University. The room was packed with graduate students from all walks of life, backgrounds, and generations. A speaker stood at the podium, lauding us for making a deliberate choice to become speech therapists. We were praised for signing up to have a career that involves the three Cs: caring, communication, and commitment—the cornerstones of human civilization. Or something to that effect. Many of the men in the room cleared their throats, smirked, or shuffled their feet, uncomfortable with the implications that this job, more than others, would put them in touch with their softer, more feminine side. As if it were a bad thing!

Many of the women in the room were nodding or unsurprised. They knew the truth already. The truth that, for many women (more so than men), part of rating overall job satisfaction and pride in performance involves calibrating how much of a positive impact they have on community.

That's what this book is all about. It's a female perspective on entrepreneurship, through the behaviorist/educational lens of someone who's been in the trenches for both the Tech Revolution and the Entrepreneurial Revolution and has learned some survival skills worth sharing. This book is a look back, and a current map of sorts, to help point out and highlight the technology and cultural trends that impact today's professional woman. The one trying to juggle work, family, personal growth, and satisfaction with her life. More than for previous generations of women, this desire for personal satisfaction in the workplace is an inchoate longing and an attainable goal, one that so many of us strive for in the new millennium.

This book is about exploiting patterns, planning methodically, and executing specific behaviors to achieve your goals. To not only be successful and profitable but to really make a difference for others. To use your own inner landscapes and strengths—learned and innate—to build a better female entrepreneur. The one we see glimpses of in our nightly dreams and in our rearview mirror. The one we hear echoes of in our daily conversations, real or imagined, with our inner selves or with friends and family.

The NICE Reboot is for every independent-minded, creative, and curious little girl like me who grew up asking *why not* instead of *why*. For every woman who has learned so much, yet knows there is still much to learn — about life and one's purpose in it. For the professional woman with a vision who is bravely and, yes, sometimes unsuccessfully, trying to share with the world. To foster change. Because change is good. Change is needed. Now more than ever.

Why the acronym NICE? Because it encompasses my philosophy about what should be valued, emulated, and implemented in the workplace. Having never been a man (although I do sometimes wonder about my previous life!), I cannot claim an understanding of the male psyche. Having been born a female, growing up in the United States, in the shadow of *E.T.* and the hostage crisis behind the film *Argo,* witnessing the birth of Apple, the Internet, NASA's dream of an International Space Station coming true, as well as the fall of communism, the Berlin Wall, the Twin Towers, and Wall Street, I feel that the spirit of reinventing oneself, of innovation, of entrepreneurship, is alive and well and calling our names. This spirit, especially for today's women, can be summed up with this acronym: NICE. It stands for:

N = Nice

I = Informed

C = Competent

E = Entrepreneurial

In the ensuing chapters, I will share my blueprint for best practices and my survival-kit-style tips for making you a better female entrepreneur in today's startup culture. I will do so in four steps, touching on skill sets we already have and suggesting that we engage in specific practical and psychological behaviors to inculcate new ones. Like a pirate's map, this book is meant to illuminate paths to achieving your own professional goals, with the understanding that your plans *can and will change.* Like a child's drawing, it's a work in progress; as I am, as many of us are and secretly hope to remain. That's the essence of being human, being a lifelong student, and being versatile, especially in today's tech-centric, currency-driven, and rapidly changing global market.

This guidebook is for today's female entrepreneur, or an aspiring one, who is bold, curious, multiculturally aware, and technologically inclined. It's designed to provide the uninitiated with practical examples and strategies and the initiated with online sources, suggested bibliographies, a different psychological perspective, and deliberate questions and quotes to ponder. I hope to enrich all of your best practices and to enhance your understanding of the philosophy behind those best practices. It's my goal to inspire you to become a more practical, well-rounded, humane, and balanced entrepreneur.

Anna Sewell, author of *Black Beauty,* said, "I write about what I know." This book is a culmination of what I've learned — about entrepreneurship, about retaining your humanity, about fostering your passion and playfulness in the face of today's mentally, spiritually, and physically grinding workplace. It's about heeding the inner voices we sometimes ignore. The ones in our minds and in our souls.

Thank you for letting me accompany you on your journey and for taking the time to read this book. I sincerely wish you the best of luck navigating your own path. I hope that the experiences you have on the way become blueprints for other women to follow and learn from. We owe it to the Sisterhood, past, present, and future. Let's pay it forward and watch nice things happen, information flow, competence increase, and entrepreneurship flourish. Let the games begin! May you all be winners of both the tangible and intangible prizes in life. And don't forget to enjoy the ride.

ONE

Getting Started

N = NICE

Gardner's Multiple Intelligences and Implications

KEY WEBSITES

- http://bit.ly/gardner-multiple-intelligences
- http://bit.ly/find-your-strengths
- http://bit.ly/bgfl-multiple-intelligences
- http://bit.ly/learning-styles
- http://bit.ly/mbti-personality-types

Quotes to Ponder

The woman who thinks she is intelligent, demands equal rights with men.

— Sidonie Gabrielle Colette

Anything that is worth teaching can be presented in many different ways. These multiple ways can make use of our multiple intelligences.

— Dr. Howard Gardner

Definition

THE THEORY OF *multiple intelligences* suggests that people have various learning styles that affect their intake of information from their five senses (perceiving and processing), and integrate that information with what they already know, store, or remember from events they previously experienced. This information is then paired with the vocabulary associated with that event.

Neuropsychologists call this *episodic memory,* a byproduct of a person's executive functioning skills. Episodic memory is what's responsible for our behavior when we find ourselves out of our element or dealing with the same unwanted situation when we dig into our stored memories of past events and snippets of vocabulary to help us contextually make sense of our current predicament. We use our learned knowledge to navigate uncharted waters — socially, mentally, and even physically. This behavior is learned over time, and our learning styles help feed our episodic memory. So it's crucial for you to be aware of what it is that you're remembering and how it's getting into your memory banks in the first place. Dr. Howard Gardner, a developmental psychologist at Harvard, posited the theory of multiple intelligences in 1983. He stated that you have seven learning styles (some say eight) that affect your cognition (your ability to perceive, recognize, conceive, and reason), your rate and depth of learning, your behavior, and your overall performance or competence.

It's important for entrepreneurs to understand these different learning styles because that understanding gives you insight into the way you perceive, process, and retain memories of how the world works and your role in it. It helps you better master your approach to problem solving and how you pitch your products or services. It helps you more clearly grasp your project collaborators' and/or customers' inner landscapes and any potential pitfalls you might encounter when being asked to respond to a call to action. Educators have long known that learning styles affect your inner landscape, and that they fall into three main categories: auditory, visual, and tactile. What is interesting about Dr. Gardner's research is that it revealed that these three styles contain subcategories that can show cross-pollination in the way the brain learns and retains information about your environment and those in it.

Multiple Intelligences — Traits and Implications

THE IMPLICATIONS OF the concept of multiple intelligences for entrepreneurs are huge (see my pointers below). To help you see the value in understanding the concept here is the list of the eight types of intelligences for you to use as a self-assessment tool to facilitate introspection and self-realization. At the very least, you can use what you've learned as a great conversation starter at your next meeting or interview!

⊛ **Kinesthetic** (Tactile Learning/Body Awareness): craves touch and sensory input from different textures of clothes and food, etc., so work environment (surroundings, furnishings) is important as well as athletic outlets for stress management, etc.

⊛ **Visuo-Spatial** (Visual Learning/Gestalt Awareness): creative, artistic, sees the big picture, good at determining project trajectories and division of labor for projects; work environment is important (surroundings, furnishings)

⊛ **Rhythmic** (Musical Learning): sensitive to mood, time-sequenced movements, and tempos of people and places; good at time management and forestalling missed deadlines for projects; thrives on timed activities, especially when paired with music

⊛ **Verbal/Linguistic** (Auditory Learning): good retention of vocabulary; a wordsmith; good debating, oration, and literacy skills; gravitates toward providing oral presentations and social media marketing campaigns; thrives on conversation or brainstorming in the workplace

⊛ **Naturalist** (Detail-Oriented): adventurous; craves open spaces and the great outdoors; sees connections or patterns in nature and in living things; gravitates toward nature, telecommuting, and travel opportunities in the workplace and toward people who are Kinesthetic

⊛ **Logical** (Analytical): math-oriented; detail-oriented; good reasoning skills; sequential thinker; bottom-line or outcome thinker for projects requiring multiple team players and multiple goals or products to be restructured, reshuffled, and reassigned; gravitates toward Visuo-Spatial people

⊛ **Intrapersonal** (Self-Awareness): understands own theory of mind and drives; encompasses what educators would call metacognition and executive functioning; introspective, reflective, sensitive, and contained; a good listener; gravitates toward taking on a series of tasks that will be thoughtfully completed with extra small touches; tends to like some quiet "me" time to complete tasks

⊛ **Interpersonal** (Social): empathetic; intuitive to others' needs and wants; charismatic; enjoys group activities; gravitates toward leadership, supervisory, or managerial roles in the workplace and toward people who are Verbal/ Linguistic

Years ago an interesting book was published that provided the lay person with insight and self-awareness about episodic memory, learning style, and theory of mind (a term coined by neuropsychologists that refers to your perspective and empathy). The book, in quiz form, relies on your learned vocabulary and stored memories along with practical aspects of the *Theory of Multiple Intelligences* to answer existential questions about your search for meaning and a sense of belonging in an increasingly disconnected and confusing world. It made the rounds in universities, coffee shops, singles events featuring speed-dating, and neighborhood book clubs. Women in particular were fascinated by *The Cube* by Annie Gottlieb and Slobodan Pesic. It's a great example of outside-the-box thinking about relationships, communication, and human nature. I read it, took the quiz, and learned a lot about myself — things that have helped me as an entrepreneur and public speaker today. I challenge you to get the book (probably not in bookstores, but Amazon has it for roughly $10) and take the quiz, individually or as a group if you don't mind sharing how your mind works! It's on my favorites list and keeper shelf, and I've dusted it off and used it quite a bit to self-evaluate and to mentor others at various points in my career. Try it, and see what I mean!

Penina's Pointers

Multiple Intelligences — Implications for Entrepreneurs

The nature vs. nurture debate heated up when Dr. Gardner published his MI theory in *Frames of Mind*. There was much interest in his work, especially in education and business. The term *multiple intelligences* has since become a buzzword, signifying your inner landscape that's shaped by the intrinsic, internal traits you're either born with, you've honed over time, or both.

MI reflects what you bring to the table when going through school, applying for a job, completing projects, or contributing to the community at large. Learning styles play a significant role:

- When you implement goals and choose the right tool from your toolbox

- When you react to sudden changes in your environment

- When you recognize and appreciate another's performance (whether it be tangible, such as currency vs. being paid in desserts, or intangible, such as verbal praise)

- When you choose your career path (what you gravitate toward)

- When you react to obstacles, challenges, and setbacks in your professional or personal voyage to greener pastures

You must consider your own learning styles and those of others (and how they may differ) when thinking about how to get ahead in business, help others, or influence another human being's perspective, say during a sales pitch. A YouTube video clip I like that points out differences between people is the Heineken beer commercial featuring "his" and "her" closets (http://bit.ly/heineken-commercial).

Our learning style affects our perceptions, reactions, and recollections about the world around us and those in it. It influences our choices in life — from friends to collaborators at work, from the way we feather our nest at home to the type of outdoor leisure activity we engage in. I believe that our learning style is inborn but gets honed over time and space. It reveals itself in our personal credo and our work mantra, in our hazy childhood memories and our recent conversations with family. Which brings me to my next point...

What's On Your Tombstone?
Leaving a Legacy Behind

KEY WEBSITES

- ⌐ http://bit.ly/helping-others-makes-us-happy
- ⌐ http://bit.ly/does-volunteering-help-anyone
- ⌐ http://bit.ly/psychology-of-volunteering
- ⌐ http://bit.ly/health-benefits-of-volunteering

Quotes to Ponder

It's only when we truly know and understand that we have a limited time on earth, we will then begin to live each day to the fullest.

— Elizabeth Kübler-Ross

The things you do for yourself are gone when you are gone, but the things you do for others remain as your legacy.

— Kalu Kalu

Definition

Legacy: Something transmitted by or received from an ancestor or predecessor or from the past.

— *The Merriam-Webster Dictionary*

WHEN YOU HEAR the word *legacy,* what comes to mind? Something left to you in a will? Teachings and thought leadership lessons that live on, long after the person is gone? Is a legacy tangible or intangible, and why does it matter? Many people today think of a legacy as something tangible. There's an increasing tendency in our youths, especially in Western countries and industrial cultures, to think in terms of "stuff." Amassing stuff — household items, gadgets, and money. I'm not saying money is irrelevant or unimportant. I'm just saying that if you're becoming an entrepreneur to make money quickly and easily, you're in for a rude awakening, especially in this economy! The Great Recession has certainly dented our morale and our ability to leave a legacy for future generations, tangible or intangible. Materialism, altruism, and industrialism have all undergone massive changes in recent years. Some of the lessons and codes of conduct handed down to the next generation no longer apply or will be outdated in another few years or so. The nature of our legacies has been affected. Our economy has been affected. Our collective mood has been affected. And our philanthropic tendencies have certainly been affected.

In the years after the Civil War, when many people came to terms with lives lost, a way of life discontinued, and the need to rethink their plans, there was a huge push, a migration, to settle the untamed Western frontier. A common question was then asked — in saloons, wagon trains, and farms; of family and friends, strangers and neighbors — "What's on your tombstone?"

The question is a valid one. It makes you think: How do you want to be remembered? Leaving a legacy behind is not just a religious, cultural, legal, or business aspiration. So if your days were numbered, what would you want to focus on? I've been thinking of this a lot since I lost my best friend and mentor to cancer and since I became an entrepreneur during one of the worst and longest recessions in recent years. It's something Steve Jobs seemed to have thought about too in preparation for giving the commencement speech at Stanford University in 2005. He said, "Remembering that I'll be dead soon is the most important tool I've ever encountered to help me make the big choices in life. Because almost everything — all external expectations, all pride, all fear of embarrassment or failure — these things just fall away in the face of death, leaving only what is truly important."

A legacy involves having an impact on others. In 2007 the Corporation for National and Community Service published a report entitled *The Health Benefits of Volunteering*. In it, research findings were reported linking increased physical health and acts of volunteering. "While it is undoubtedly the case that better health leads to continued volunteering, these studies demonstrate that volunteering also leads to improved physical and mental health. Thus they are part of a self-reinforcing cycle."

Volunteering and philanthropy are important in entrepreneurship because they help you maintain emotional equilibrium, happiness, health, and legacy-building behaviors. Not to mention that they give you opportunities to network and practice communication and other skills as well. In July 2013 Bruce DeBoskey, a consultant and strategist for entrepreneurial philanthropy based in Colorado, wrote an article (http://bit.ly/startups-include-philanthropy) that makes a case for my concept of a legacy and for the creation of nonprofit advisory boards within existing entrepreneurial business models. He wrote, "By inserting philanthropy into the very DNA of a startup, entrepreneurs make community engagement an organic part of the organization."

But looking at legacies and volunteering through my NICE lens has made me realize that you can use advisory boards, mentors, and structured moments of giving back to help create a psychological legacy. I want to point out that altruism and volunteer work need not be structured activities all the time. I believe that volunteer work and a desire to give back is part of a person's legacy. That today engaging in meaningful, humane, and helpful content curation using social media is a form of volunteering. Staying late at work to complete reports that will benefit others is a form of volunteering. Lending a listening ear and a helping hand amid trying to complete your own to-do list is a form of volunteering. Caring about and promoting sustainability of our resources for the betterment of the environment is a form of volunteering. All contribute to your legacy, your legacy of deeds.

But what is a legacy, really?

As a person who believes that a human being is created in God's image, with the various multiple intelligence traits to inculcate and implement, I ponder this question a lot. I reflect on the concept of a psychic and psycho-social legacy, stemming from the use of one's own talents and contributions to others. Being nice, in the truest sense of the word, means implementing social reform. It means striving for greater achievements and increased performance of feats, small and large, to enrich the lives of others and provide sustainability of our planet for future generations. It means being responsible and accountable for engaging in entrepreneurial efforts that will impact upon innovation of humanitarian efforts, not just global markets and revenue.

I believe that the journey of entrepreneurship, filled with challenges that are ethical, psychological, and spiritual, requires us to ask that question of ourselves — What is a legacy, really? Women in general, female educators, and mothers in particular (being the ones who biologically give birth) are in a great position to nurture and influence children's moral and intellectual compasses. It's in our female DNA to grow, nurture, and care about the welfare of our children and their children. We are hard-wired to measure overall job satisfaction and pride in our performance by calibrating how much of a positive impact we have on our community, not just ourselves.

We are thus particularly receptive to being sensitive to this version of the concept of a legacy. No one can pinpoint the exact moment when a child sees someone do or say something that may be felt decades later. No one can discount the importance of giving back, contributing to the world somehow in altruistic and sustainable manners, to make it a better place for future generations.

I propose that female entrepreneurs, possessing a neuropsychological skill set that renders us nice and nurturing, among other valuable traits, are in a unique position to leave a meaningful legacy behind, physically and metaphysically. A legacy that has the ability to be self-sustaining and promote change. A legacy that enables others to plot the course of their trajectory, to continue fostering a culture of sustainability, kindness, and giving. That culture is in danger of being extinguished in today's somewhat narcissistic, survivor-mentality culture that is steadily permeating the way we conduct ourselves, in business and in life.

Altruism, paying it forward, philanthropy, and even sustainability (such as recycling and not littering) are deliberate behaviors that require only minutes of time for us to feel effects that can last for hours, days, or years. Kindness can be verbally and nonverbally demonstrated, quickly! The way we as entrepreneurs talk to employees, potential clients, competitors, and people we meet in our travels is just as crucial as what we do philanthropically. I've made mistakes like other novices and have learned to analyze the *why* (triggers) and increase the *what now* (apologize, change course or strategy).

In the book *Made to Stick,* authors Dan and Chip Heath argue the case for using stories to make your message stick. I'll refer in depth to that book later on, but for now I want you to think about the concept of a story and how it makes a legacy stick. Part of leaving a legacy behind, one that's remembered and valued, involves taking part in (contributing to and sharing the story of) other people's lives. That's why storytelling is so valued. It touches on our quest for immortality, starting with our childhood fascination with tales. It helps us bequeath a psychic and socio-emotional legacy for those we care about. That's why it's such a time-honored tradition in Native American and aboriginal tribes.

The best stories grab our attention and theory of mind (empathy, perspective) from the start, in essence freezing time and allowing us to really harness it by living in the moment. In essence stories develop your theory of mind and group-think tendencies, which is why digital marketing and entrepreneurial gurus now advocate for story integration. That's why a type of storytelling, visual digitalization using videos and photos in social media marketing campaigns to forge an emotional connection with the customer, is now painstakingly taught to entrepreneurs. For an in-depth example read pages 172–78 in *Business Model Generation* by Alexander Osterwalder, Yves Pigneur, et al. This groundbreaking book, which I highly recommend, gives you a blueprint for various storytelling techniques, from using visual cues (slideshows, video clips, comic strips, photos) to publicly role playing the protagonist's problem-solving techniques in an interactive way (as you do in the game charades).

It all boils down to one thing — causality. There's a reason we're drawn to stories. At the end of the day, human beings are all struggling to harness time, make it work for us, and restructure the causality loop of our own choices and actions and its impact on our story. The story of the hero's journey, written about so eloquently by Joseph Campbell in *The Hero With a Thousand Faces,* resonates with this struggle and allows us to collectively tap into our memory banks to recall similar events or feelings we may have experienced and how the outcomes aligned or didn't. We're then spurred to change our behavior, which affects the trajectory of the behaviors of others.

The point I'm making is that a legacy is more than an object we leave behind in a will. A legacy is the result of our attempts to cognitively and deliberately string together moments of time. How? By leading by example while we're living and by leaving an existential blueprint comprising our actions and stories to follow when we're gone. I like to think it's what prompted one of our greatest storytellers of all time, Mark Twain, to say, "The two most important days in your life are the day you are born and the day you find out why."

Let me give you a true story to hit this point home. I remember the first time I traveled by myself after graduate school, before Facebook and cell phones. I went to visit good friends in Iowa. I offered to help out with dinner and was asked to go grocery shopping. Remember, this was before the Internet, smart phones, and social media. Without arming myself with tips about this store (as people do today with Yelp and Trip Advisor apps or even Angie's List), I braved the supermarket with its unfamiliar aisles and protocols. As I paid for my purchases, a teenage boy, only a few years younger than me, wheeled out my bags past the store's exit. Not knowing where and why he headed out, I chased after him yelling, in true New York tough-city-girl fashion, "Hey you, those are my groceries you're stealing!" He turned around, literally ran back, and collided with several other people who were tripping over themselves to assure me that, no, he was going to meet me at my car and actually place all the bags in the trunk. For free. Right now. And not only for me. He does it for everyone who shops in the store. No matter what. I was shocked. The novice traveler and Manhattan girl in me was floored.

I apologized profusely to the still-smiling boy, who did indeed transfer my groceries to my car's trunk as promised. With a smile and a "here you go, miss." He even refused a tip. Kindness, quick and painless, but it resonated with me for years. He was raised right, and he didn't get mad at my outburst or sulk. I remembered his actions for years. More importantly, they reflected well on his family and place of employment. I recommended that store to other people in the neighborhood. Too bad this was before the days of the Internet. I could have used social media to praise and promote that boy and his future endeavors as well as the supermarket that gave him his start.

Being nice. It's more than just a personality trait. It's a practiced, intentional behavior and an outlook about life. About how to treat those who cross your path while you're living it.

Fast forward to 2013. Another true story. In February, on a domestic flight from Texas to New York, I had an opportunity to pay it forward, which thankfully I didn't blow. I was on my way back home, on a crowded flight, right after giving a seminar to a large group of educators in a specific school district about the developmental integration of iPad apps into lesson plans for young children with autism and special needs. I had taken out my iPad and was focused on my screen. The woman sitting next to me leaned in and stared at my screen. She kept staring. I decided not to ignore her, despite my looming deadline to submit an article or proposal or such, and began chatting with her. I did a quick show and tell session where I scrolled through various pages of app folders, demonstrating various apps. As the woman saw me turn to page four, then five, all filled with folders of apps, her eyes widened. She looked at me and said, "Excuse me, but I have to ask: Are you a speech therapist?"

She then informed me who she was (also a speech therapist, Shannon Benton MS/CCC-SLP, founder and Executive Director of CLASP International), and we got to talking. She showed me the brochures she had made to distribute at a fundraising dinner she was attending that evening. I asked for a few to distribute at my next seminar. We talked about her organization, and I found myself telling her about mine. The next thing I knew, I donated several free promo codes for my Socially Speaking™ iPad App, which is a social skills development assessment protocol that's fully customizable. Since her work takes her to culturally diverse places such as Zambia and Kenya, she was very interested in new, customizable techniques and products. I then offered to train or mentor her team members, despite that little voice in my head (the one coming from the harried woman with the dollar sign hat who always frowns at me), and the next thing I knew I was training and consulting with the staff at CLASP International's Autism Clinic and loving it. Still am.

One drop raises the sea. One act of kindness, one kind phrase or affirmation, can change your path and the path of countless children you may one day help. Even if you're not an educationally based entrepreneur like myself.

There's an essay I hung on my speech therapy office wall for years, which now hangs in my home. It was a gift from my best friend and mentor, which I read every day. It's a famous poem entitled "A Hundred Years From Now," which I would like to share. I hope you'll take these words to heart and add philanthropy and legacy to your entrepreneur's to-do list like I did. This essay has become one of my daily mantras and is deeply engraved on the compass of my soul:

One hundred years from now
It will not matter
What kind of car I drove,
What kind of house I lived in,
How much I had in my bank
Nor what my clothes looked like.
…
But the world may be …
a little better because …
I was important in the life of a child.

Mission Statement Guidelines and Online Resources

KEY WEBSITES

- http://bit.ly/how-to-write-a-mission-statement
- http://bit.ly/mission-and-vision-statements
- http://bit.ly/how-to-write-a-program-mission-statement
- http://bit.ly/how-to-write-a-powerful-mission-statement

Quotes to Ponder

I remember thinking, I'll just keep doing this as long as I can get away with it.

— Tina Fey

Everyone has his own specific vocation or mission in life ... everyone's task is unique as his specific opportunity to implement it.

— Dr. Viktor E. Frankl

Definition

MISSION STATEMENTS are defined as written words about your company's soul and role on this earth. Your mission statement should define your purpose as an entrepreneur, inspire people to join your figurative call to action, and create traffic to your social media sites. The wording should be long enough to help you create a digital footprint, yet short enough to give people a quick insight into what you and your company stand for regarding your services or products.

I read a wonderfully practical, surprisingly funny book in my early days as a startup, bootstrapping entrepreneur that really made me think. It made me think about the mental and emotional cubicles we put ourselves in. It made me ponder my goals and gave me a different perspective about the components of my mission. I'm talking about Pamela Slim's *Escape From Cubicle Nation*. I want to quote from it, but find myself recommending the entire Chapter 3 instead. I want to point out that her suggestion to create a vision board is genius. Slim advocates that you start your brainstorming process by taking your own drawings, mementos, and photos of things that catch your fancy and cut-outs and clippings from magazines to create a graphic representation comprising words and images related to your topic of interest. A literal, tangible picture of your inner landscape — a mind map of your stored memories and your chi.

Vision boards aren't new to me. They're something that the world of education, particularly special education involving children with autism (who have been proven to be predominantly visual learners), have used for a while. They're something that the insightful, sensitive oncology nurses told my best friend, the determined, reflective scholar who was battling cancer, to use. A vision board, at its core, is an easy to see and maintain representation of your goals, long term and short, and the steps you need to take to achieve them.

Lately, many people in corporate settings, in marketing and in incubators and/or accelerators, have offhandedly remarked (either to me in person or online in social media posts) that they use the wording of their initial elevator pitches (whether for interviews or to snag projects or venture capital or crowdfunding) as a basis for the wording they use in their raisons d'être — their mantras and their mission statements. For their websites and for their companies. Having used a vision board as an introductory, opening salvo for tasks I needed to break down or as a time-management strategy when completing projects in the education and healthcare arenas with human beings I actually know (not just showing off my plethora of photos or

If I see it, I understand it.....
- Dr. Temple Grandin

"When humor goes, there goes civilization."
- Erma Bombeck

One hundred years from now
It will not matter
What kind of car I drove,
What kind of house I lived in,
How much I had in my bank
Nor what my clothes looked like.
But the world may be
a little better because,
I was important in the life of a child

Penina's Vision Board 2013

"Instead of Thinking Outside the Box,
Get Rid of the Box!"
- Deepak Chopra

LIFE IS ABOUT USING THE WHOLE BOX OF CRAYONS

"Alone we can do so little, together we can do so much."
- Helen Keller

Life's a Journey, Enjoy the Ride!

"Trust that the dots will somehow connect in your future."
- Steve Jobs

Think Different!

I *Can* and I Will....Watch *Me*!

Figure 1-1. Penina's vision board. This is a section from Penina's vision board that offers a visual representation of her corporate mission.

my slideshow to investors or venture capitalists who may be captive, faceless receptacles of my hook at meetings or during webinars), I see things differently and respectfully disagree with them.

You should develop your mission statement first, before you have an elevator pitch. Patiently. Methodically. Visually. Visually break down your concepts to their most basic components. You'll surprise yourself with your focus, with insights about elements of design that you may not have considered and, most of all, with your ability to plot a course of action that's more sequential than you expected. Everything else that you do for your business that you look at as the next link in the chain will be viewed through the lens of your mission. Developing your mission statement first will change the way you approach your projects, pitch, and players. It will change the way you react to events beyond your control. Try it, and see what I mean.

Penina's Pointers
Three Tips for Writing a Mission Statement

1. **Brainstorm with your inner voice and those you trust.** Try to understand the contribution you want to make. Determine your values, strengths, and other important aspects of yourself. To get the brainstorming process started, analyze yourself, your raison d'être, and ask others who know you well how they perceive your role in life, in your job, in your community, and in your family. Look online for examples, such as this post I found on Wendy Maynard's *Kinesis Blog:* http://bit.ly/how-to-write-a-powerful-mission-statement. Here are some examples of powerful mission statements that she cited:

- ⚙ **Amazon:** *To be the most customer-centric company in the world, where people can find and discover anything they want to buy online.*

- ⚙ **eBay:** *Provide a global trading platform where practically anyone can trade practically anything.*

- ⚙ **Nike:** *To bring inspiration and innovation to every athlete in the world.*

- ⚙ **Starbucks:** *To inspire and nurture the human spirit — one person, one cup and one neighborhood at a time.*

2. **Keep the three strikes rule.** Write your first draft, then a second, and then a third. Keep your drafts short, using words that evoke inspiration, action, and focus. Make a vision board using real photos and newspaper clippings, or keep it digital and green. Use an app to design a poster and an app for your portfolio to save items to paste in order to gain clarity (I use Evernote and Pocket for my iPad). Make mistakes; leave your draft and go do something else. For a whole day and night. Sleep on it. Then come back to it, to flesh it out some more. Write it in shorthand using an app on a mobile device for easy access and revisions on the go. I like to use the iOS app Tree Notepad because it separates the title from the body of the note, forcing me to really think!

3. **Publicize your mission.** Post it online to make it part of your digital footprint. Post it, or information about it, on your newly created digital platform using Facebook, Pinterest, Google+, YouTube, Tumblr, and website pages. Connect the dots. If you play your cards right, it'll stick. Your mission will then become part of your brand.

Business Plan Guidelines

KEY WEBSITES

- ⌐ http://bit.ly/how-to-write-a-business-plan
- ⌐ http://bit.ly/sample-business-plans
- ⌐ http://bit.ly/starting-a-business
- ⌐ http://bit.ly/business-resources
- ⌐ http://bit.ly/keeping-financial-documents

Quotes to Ponder

Nothing will work unless you do.

— Maya Angelou

Efficiency is doing things right; effectiveness is doing the right things.

— Peter Drucker

Definition

IN AS FEW WORDS as possible a *business plan* provides the most essential information about you and your services or products. Different entrepreneurship opportunities require different formats, such as pitching your business using a short digital slideshow (about 10 slides), e-mailing customized proposals written for a job interview prior to the interview, completing all the areas of a LinkedIn profile, or just writing an expanded mission statement to present to others. A good business plan includes clear correlations between your ability to solve problems in the real world and your course of action, including a money trail, to solve those problems.

Recently there's been much debate in the literature about the efficacy of a formal business plan and how long and detailed it has to be. I believe it's important, but there's wiggle room in how formally it needs to be drawn up and proposed. I've found it extremely helpful to read and study, in depth, the fantastic specifications for different business plans that are depicted visually and creatively (which really appealed to me!) in the grassroots effort turned mega-hit book *Business Model Generation* by Alexander Osterwalder, Yves Pigneur, et al. I write et al because the book was co-written and digitally collaborated on by "an amazing crowd of 470 practitioners from 45 countries," all of whom helped the authors create "a handbook for visionaries, game changers, and challengers striving to defy outdated business models and design tomorrow's enterprises." The words speak for themselves, and those are just from the cover. Imagine what you learn when actually opening the book! I put that book on my keeper shelf and recommend that you do so as well.

When delving into this rich, strategy-packed book that reads like a cross between an architectural draft and furniture assembly instructions from Ikea (only much more visually clear and linear), I couldn't help but notice that this book referred to much more than a business plan. It showcased and gave advice about an entrepreneur's potential blindside — the business model environment (context, design drivers, and constraints). An entrepreneur, especially a startup and a bootstrapping one at that, has no choice but to wear many hats to launch the service or product that puts her company on the map, especially the digital map. But how many times do we find that the hats don't really fit, or that they keep falling off? That is, how often do we neglect factors on the periphery of the business plan that can make it or break it? This book brilliantly highlights the various pieces of the puzzle, the patterns that an entrepreneur needs to consider. The book is now available for print purchase, and I cannot recommend the business model environment chapter starting on page 200 enough.

In a nutshell, the book discusses a four-phase business model from which to derive your business plan. It lists the business model environment's three key elements: context, design drivers, and constraints. It then suggests that the new business model is all about perceiving your "design space" as an octopus with four tentacles, which are roughly mapped out as follows:

1. **Market forces** (customer needs and leads, branding, costs and strategies to keep them, etc.)

2. **Industry forces** (competitors and stakeholders, thought leadership trends, etc.)

3. **Key trends-foresight** (disruptive innovation, cultural and socio-economic trends, etc.)

4. **Macroeconomic forces** (global and capital market conditions, public economic infrastructure affecting consumer sustainability and quality of life, etc.)

I also recommend that you take a look at *Playing to Win* by A. G. Wafley and Roger Martin, especially page 212. That page lists components of winning in business, which I believe actually form the metalinguistic components of the words used in successful, effective, easy-to-understand, and easily implemented business plans. The authors ask readers to ponder five questions to help them plot a course of action. Let me paraphrase them as statements, interpreted through my NICE lens:

1. **Draft your business plan.** Clearly define what winning means to you, the entrepreneur.

2. **Stick to your business plan.** Decide where to play to win and which venues to avoid.

3. **Formulate the how of your business plan.** Determine the ways you will play to win when you engage.

4. **Execute your business plan** (the best you can using what you've learned). Make choices as to what to keep and discard, according to your own knowledge and what conventional wisdom deems best practices.

5. **Manage your business plan.** Support steps 1 to 4 wisely using traditional marketing, social media, mentors, and capital.

Penina's Pointers

What to Include in Your Business Plan

1. **The Problem:** What you feel needs to be addressed to help enrich the lives of others.

2. **The Solution:** Why you are the right person to address this issue, and how you intend to do so.

3. **The Timeline:** Current events affecting your efficacy to be a fixer of this problem, and moments in history (professional and environmental) leading up to this moment when you are stepping forward to provide a service or product.

4. **The Who's Who List:** Names, titles, and roles of other team players, if applicable (be nice — make sure to list some adjectives in their job description), and don't forget to add who your target audience is!

Why Incorporate, and How to Do It Online

KEY WEBSITES

- ⌐ http://bit.ly/incorporation-primer
- ⌐ http://bit.ly/forming-a-corporation
- ⌐ http://bit.ly/why-incorporate

Quotes to Ponder

A woman is like a tea bag; you can't tell how strong she is until you put her in hot water.

— Eleanor Roosevelt

So many dot-com companies were formulated on air.

— William Shatner

Definition

A BEST PRACTICE is a technique that consistently shows results superior to those achieved by other means. Using best practices is critical in many areas of business. Best practices are especially important in the personal branding of your service or product, personal asset protection if sued, and tax breaks involving deductible expenses. Here's a best practice that will help you be successful in these areas: create a new corporation (in my case I created a limited liability company named Socially Speaking™ LLC) under the governing laws of the state you live in. Incorporating can help you reap many benefits.

I'm not an accountant, nor do I work for the IRS. In 2010 I was in the dark like many employees who turned to self-employment and realized the need to incorporate. I needed to learn about incorporating quickly, especially because of the Great Recession (more on that later). Seasoned entrepreneurs told me to speak to my accountant and just swallow the consulting fee (unless the accountant is kind and takes pity on the clueless client, which happened to me). Newly minted entrepreneurs from generation Y, also known as the millennial generation (more on them later, including why an entrepreneur needs to learn from them), told me to search online.

Since I'm an educator and techie, Google has long been my friend, and Bing and the later-launched Dolphin for iPad were becoming more than passing acquaintances. But I was still a skeptic. Boy was I in for an epiphany! Not only did I learn *how* to do it myself but I learned *where* to go online to get it done! I used Nolo.com, which gave me online tech support and phone support and filed the paperwork for me with the state in which I lived and practiced. That's when it dawned on me that more women can get in on the fun. We could start our own businesses easily and cheaply and take steps to keep them financially sound. That lesson stayed with me and started me on the road that took me here, to write this chapter, for other readers searching for answers.

Penina's Pointers

Incorporate Online Using One of These Websites

1. **Nolo:** http://bit.ly/form-an-llc-online (I used this one)

2. **The Company Corporation:** http://bit.ly/incorporate-today

Reminders to Help You Avoid Problems in Setting Up Your Corporation

⊛ The type of company you start, how you incorporate it, and what your expenses are will *all* determine the kinds of federal tax breaks you'll be entitled to. Search online. Take books out of the library. Ask your bank questions. Talk to your accountant. Get further information and file it away.

⊛ If your service or product involves the distribution of your own written, drawn, recorded, produced, or created material (like my Socially Speaking™ iPad App), you need to copyright and possibly trademark your work, *all* of it, as your own intellectual property, specifically using a *patent* lawyer. The day legal action can be taken by a jack-of-all-trades is long gone. Pay an expert now with money, or pay later with frustrated tears and stress. Your choice. The "fake it until you make it" line is just that, a line. Need proof? Read this article: http://bit.ly/faking-it-is-bad-business.

⊛ Once you've incorporated, you'll need to get your tax ID# (EIN) and business certificates — make copies, file them, and then hang up this information on a wall *where you do business* so others can see! That includes bylaws and possibly employee-related information. You can search online, including the two websites I listed above, for further information.

Tax Breaks for Entrepreneurs
Deductible Expenses for the Self-Employed

KEY WEBSITES

- 🖱 http://bit.ly/IRS-self-employed-tax-center
- 🖱 http://bit.ly/IRS-business-taxes
- 🖱 http://bit.ly/IRS-deducting-business-expenses
- 🖱 http://bit.ly/what-women-must-know-about-money

Quotes to Ponder

We apply law to facts. We don't apply feelings to facts.

— Sonia Sotomayor

The hardest thing to understand in the world is the income tax.

— Albert Einstein

Definition

DISCUSSIONS OF *TAX BREAKS* can be rather dry, and while not fun they're part of an entrepreneur's maintenance, like changing the filter in a Brita water pitcher at regular intervals. Talk to your financial advisor (some banks give free consultations) or accountant about possible deductions. A tax break essentially means that you can deduct business expenses (use a business credit card so that charges are easily tracked) from the amount of money you report to the IRS when you pay your taxes (quarterly or yearly). Talk to your accountant about setting up a payment plan that's right for you. Then whenever you pay taxes, be sure to list how much you've spent that's reimbursable.

I'm at a loss about how much to disclose about entrepreneurial tax breaks, because I'm not an accountant. I also think that further detail will cause your eyes to glaze over, and we're only in Chapter 1. We haven't gotten to the good stuff yet! So I've decided to recommend again that you make use of libraries, Internet searches, friendly accountants, and helpful bank employees to answer your many questions on a case-by-case basis. I've also decided to inject humor and provide a link to Randy Glasbergen's tax cartoons. If Albert Einstein said taxes were hard to fathom, who am I to write otherwise. I make it a point to promote my company policy — educational and entertaining teachable moments. I hope I deliver on that promise in this book, but especially in this chapter with this link: http://bit.ly/funny-tax-comics.

Penina's Pointers
Your Top 10 Tax Deductions

1. Office space cost for your business, be it an actual room in the abode where you live and pay a mortgage (apartment, house) or if you rent office space elsewhere

2. Office supplies (paper, pens, stickies, stapler, etc.), computer equipment (printer, scanner, speakers, cables, webcam, projector, cases and cables, desktop and laptop computer, mobile devices such as smart phone, tablet, iPod, etc.), and furniture for your office (desk, chair, shelves, bulletin board, filing cabinet, etc.)

3. Telephone charges related to business calls

4. Subscriptions to business-related magazines (I get *Macworld*) and online cloud storage space (I pay for extra space in Apple iCloud and Evernote)

5. Gas and mileage charges related to business trips

6. Travel expenses for business trips (air or ground transport, lodging, food, hostess gifts, etc.)

7. Insurance fees for business trips if you're self-employed and paying for it (includes travel, luggage, clothes, toiletries, and equipment coverage)

8. Social Security payments

9. Retirement funding and investments (Roth IRA, mutual funds, etc.)

10. Hiring your child (if you have one listed legally as yours) to (reasonably) work for you, *if* you are self-employed (and understand why child labor laws are enforced and that we no longer live in the Industrial Revolution!)

Your Guide to Hoarding and Discarding Financial Documents for the IRS

What to Keep for Three Years

- Bank statements
- Credit card receipts
- Store receipts for business-related purchases
- Charity-related receipts
- W2 and W9 forms, 1099 forms

What to Keep for Six Years

- Tax returns
- Payroll documentation
- Invoices for services rendered
- Tax-deductible itemizations of accrued expenses
- Marketing timelines — what was done, needs to be done (digital and print, but keep only two for built-in redundancy — any more is just clutter)

What to Keep Forever

- Intellectual property documentation for trademarks and copyrights
- Deeds to property
- Ownership titles
- Business contracts
- Business letters of formation concerning incorporation
- Diplomas
- Licenses

What to Discard

❀ Bank deposit and ATM slips

❀ Monthly bank statements

❀ Letters of intent

❀ Brochures with outdated mission statements; business cards with outdated or unused phone numbers (there's an app for that!)

❀ University transcripts and report cards (unless they have sentimental value)

❀ Outdated credit and insurance cards

Your Guide to Financial Health and Maintenance: Lessons from Suze Orman's Women & Money — Owning the Power to Control Your Destiny

1. Have a durable power of attorney for medical issues that may arise.

2. Create a living will and a backup, complete with an incapacity clause should anything happen to you.

3. Have a living trust, transfer ownership of assets to that trust, and list beneficiaries.

4. Stay out of debt! I would actually recommend that you try to stay away from venture capital as long as you can! Read Seth Godin's blogs and book, *The Bootstrapper's Bible*.

5. Invest in a Roth IRA.

6. Plan for retirement. Invest wisely.

TWO

Getting Clients

I = INFORMED

The Power of a Theme Song: Inspiring Yourself and Others

KEY WEBSITES

- http://bit.ly/video-to-MP3
- http://bit.ly/apple-itunes-music
- http://bit.ly/itunes-mac-keyboard-shortcuts
- http://bit.ly/itunes-windows-keyboard-shortcuts
- http://bit.ly/windows-media-player
- http://bit.ly/spotify-for-music
- http://bit.ly/spotify-keyboard-shortcuts
- http://bit.ly/internet-music-guide
- http://bit.ly/audio-cheat-sheet
- http://bit.ly/TV-theme-songs

✌ http://bit.ly/oliver-sacks-power-of-rhythm

✌ http://bit.ly/oliver-sacks-strokes-language-music

✌ http://bit.ly/oliver-sacks-musicophilia-book

Quotes to Ponder

I had a good loud voice, and I wasn't afraid to be goofy or zany.

— Carol Burnett

After silence, that which comes nearest to expressing the inexpressible is music.

— Aldous Huxley

Definition

Music: The art or science of combining vocal or instrumental sounds (or both) to produce beauty of form, harmony, and expression of emotion.

— *New Oxford American Dictionary*

SINCE ANCIENT TIMES, music has been an important communication tool. It conveys messages without words and transports people to their pasts with just sound. Music can be a powerful motivator when tapping into your psyche or when trying to inspire others to change or implement something new.

Consider how musical instruments (bagpipes, drums, harps, and bugles) were used in war in Scotland and in the United States to inspire soldiers in battle. History books are full of references to various musical instruments being used in battle to rally the troops, signal positions, and either mourn losses or celebrate victories. So powerful is the act of musical communion and communication that the British king George II passed the Disarming Act of 1746. In it he banned bagpipes in Scotland after Bonnie Prince Charlie and the Jacobites were defeated in the Battle of Culloden in April 1746. It wasn't until the Battle of Waterloo in 1815 that Scottish pipers from the Gordon clan in Inverness used bagpipes in battle once more (http://bit.ly/pipes-and-pipers).

The history of the United States is also full of references to fifes and drums being used in war. First used by colonists in the French and Indian War, they became even more popular with the Continental Army during the Revolutionary War. In 1798 thirty-two fifers and drummers formed the United States Marine Band. Soon after, fifes and drums became the norm for soldiers training in schools such as West Point and were used to convey messages and raise spirits, especially in the War of 1812. The bugle gained immense popularity during the Civil War, soon overtaking fifes and drums as the instrument of choice. With the invention of radio, field music was done away with, so that World War II, the Vietnam War, and wars that followed didn't have units comprising fifers and drummers.

In 1960 the Old Guard Fife and Drum Corps was established as a ceremonial corps in the U.S. Army, one that went on to perform in U.S. presidential inaugural parades and other civilian functions. In 1965 the formation of the Company of Fifers and Drummers heralded an era of historic preservation and public education about a former way of life and contributions made in the past. The company is still thriving and its growing membership attracts notice all over the world, including at the annual Fasnacht Event in Basel, Switzerland. Each year thousands of like-minded individuals gather from all over the world to participate in, re-enact, and respect time-honored traditions and appreciate talented musicians (http://bit.ly/ancient-fife-and-drum).

So music, and the artists that provide it and the connoisseurs who appreciate it, can really influence your outlook and demeanor. Consider how music is used in the media today. Multimedia content (TV and radio commercials, TV shows, movies, YouTube and Vimeo videos, etc.) uses background music to:

- Set the mood for the conveyed message to be delivered in, with a higher likelihood of sharing the message

- Tap into the collective memory banks of listeners for greater impact and spreading of the desired message

Consider how movie soundtracks make you feel. Consider the TV commercials for major brands. For example, take the videos unveiled at the June 2013 Apple Worldwide Developer's Conference Keynote Address. The pressure was on, and Apple really needed to show the public how their innovative products, artistry, and creativity all set them apart from the pack. If you listen to the first video Tim Cook showed (http://bit.ly/designed-by-apple), deploying the new mission statement for Apple, you'll hear slow, soothing music designed to make you really read and think about the unfolding message. To quote Apple: "The first thing we ask is what do we want people to feel?" The music does just that.

The Apple iPhone 5 TV ad "Photos Every Day" also uses music to tap into your emotions (http://bit.ly/photos-every-day-ad). The ad shows how easy and wonderful it is to use the phone's built-in camera to photograph and preserve moments of your life. But it's the background melody that hits the point home. It's the musical accompaniment, the crescendo and tempo, that enables you to truly internalize the message, and access it later, when hearing it in passing.

Sharing music with others can enhance the feelings of the collective, of belonging, of being part of something. It can lead to shared recollections, shared purpose, and provide a shared outlook through joint attention. It can contribute to and aid in the aversion of discord and war. Just ask children and adults involved in organized sports, choirs, and marching bands.

Music, with all its facets, often has a role in rites of passage. When? In adolescence, in that period of time when children struggle to reconcile their inner landscape with the realities of the world and of growing up. In many of her books depicting family life, especially teenage life, the famous humor columnist, writer, and ultimate mother Erma Bombeck used music to depict a rite of passage. In her hilarious *Just Wait 'Til You Have Children of Your Own,* illustrated by the gifted Bil Keane of *Family Circus* fame, she devotes an entire chapter, "Stone Age Versus Rock Age," to this depiction. In the chapter, Erma writes about catching a cold and keeping a diary for "seven days of confinement" while she's held hostage by her teenage children and their music. She recalls hearing a song, under duress, and asking her daughter about it later. Her daughter laughed and said that a song that hits the charts in the morning becomes a Golden Oldie by nightfall. At the end of the week Erma seemed to have gone a bit deaf from the decibel level of the music blaring in her house. The memories of earsplitting guitar riffs and thundering drums probably scarred poor Erma for life. This rite of passage, depicted by someone with different musical tastes, is still poignantly relevant today.

Why is it that parents and children, especially adolescent children, tend to have such divergent musical playlists? Why is there such a generation gap between the teenagers of today and those of three decades ago? The answer: episodic memory. Music evokes feelings and memories of where we were and what we were doing when we first heard that song or tune, experiences that tend to differ dramatically for parents and their children.

What's the invisible thread between music and feelings? And why is it important to you as an entrepreneur?

In his book *Musicophilia,* Dr. Oliver Sacks, the British neurologist best known for his breakthrough work with people with Parkinson's and Alzheimer's diseases, discusses the importance of music as part of the experience of being human. In his book and videos (available on YouTube), Dr. Sacks discusses adult patients who have lost their connections to reality or have lost the power of speech. They can still access music they've heard and songs they once knew, however. It appears that certain tunes "seem to touch springs of memory, or emotion, which may be completely inaccessible to them, helping them regain their identity from that time they heard that song."

What's so special about music? What's so special about musicians that we should emulate them, both as artistic individuals and as entrepreneurs?

In today's society, where individuality is encouraged, there is greater access to music of all kinds. Thanks to the advances in technology and the shrinking of the global community, there is real power in communication through music and an abundance of it for the diversified palette. Communicating through music is a useful tool that can be wielded wisely in the hands of an entrepreneur, even one who can't sing or play a note.

Dr. Sacks sums up my point in one beautiful sentence: "Professional musicians, in general, possess what most of us would regard as remarkable powers of musical imagery." He goes on to write about research that shows that people who engage in visual imagery regarding music have both the auditory cortex (language and communication) and the motor cortex (movement) in their brains stimulated. This stimulation enhances their ability to develop their inner landscape and build and store episodic memory — two components to having what is known in education and neuropsychology as a theory of mind (having perspective on and empathy for those around us).

The theory of mind is often underdeveloped in young children with autism, and this underdevelopment is one of the underlying causes of the social communication challenges we try to help them overcome. This trait is often overdeveloped in the best entrepreneurs. If it's not overdeveloped, or at least adequate, then the entrepreneur needs to learn how to develop this trait. Or outsource it — hire or collaborate with people who have this trait in spades.

A good entrepreneur knows how to evoke feelings and memories in self and in others and how to better express those feelings when gearing up to do work, complete projects, pitch a service or product, or invoke change. Just go online and watch some of the speakers giving a TED talk or some of the clever TV commercials going viral on YouTube or Vimeo.

Many young children with autism have social communication challenges that involve recalling and expressing feelings inappropriately (having tantrums). I've seen the power of music in evoking feelings. I've staunchly recommended music-based activities in lesson plans, and even group music therapy, as part of the course of treatment. I've recommended that the graduate students I mentored take a music break to help reboot after a particularly stressful therapy session with a non-compliant child.

My philosophy on the power of music can be applied to entrepreneurship as follows:

1. **Feelings can be experienced on different levels simultaneously,** like a collage of various materials, or like different instruments multilayered in a song. Music helps you develop multiple intelligences and weave mosaic tapestries of past memories, both of which are needed when problem solving as an entrepreneur.

2. **Feelings can vary in intensity,** like a brushstroke on canvas, or like changing tempos in a song. Teamwork ebbs and flows in a similar fashion. A good entrepreneur knows when to be a lone wolf and when to join the pack.

3. **Feelings can be expressed in a diverse manner,** like different colors of the rainbow, a solo versus a duet, or a lone bagpipe versus a trio of violins. I especially like to use "different shades in the rainbow" or "various instruments in the orchestra" analogies when assigning specific tasks to people doing a project as a team or when I'm mentoring others.

4. **Feelings can be individualized and interpreted,** like any good painting or musical composition. Echoes of heard

music help a good entrepreneur to be more creative, develop self-concept, and be more intuitive when trying to accommodate the viewpoint of the other parties involved in the business venture.

5. **Feelings can be expressed verbally and nonverbally through body language.** Music facilitates your self-regulation. Music facilitates emotional attunement through engaging your brain's ability to perceive the tempo of feelings. Being an entrepreneur can be quite stressful, and having an outlet is important. Relaxing music can actually alleviate stress by helping to relax tense shoulders and smooth out frowning, tight facial muscles.

6. **Feelings are time sensitive, like music,** which is all about the performance of time-sequenced movements — rhythm. Music facilitates your motoric tempo, your body rhythm and timing, thereby fostering better body awareness — the awareness of an internal body clock. This awareness can help with your ability to engage in time-sensitive discussions with others (such as discussions about a raise) and to respect personal boundaries (physical and mental) more appropriately in the workplace. It can help foster emotional resonance and engagement with others.

Music is thus one of the key manners in which human beings express feelings, develop and share memories, and build bonds — music increases emotional attunement. What does this mean for an entrepreneur? It means that using music for your pitch and your presentations can bond you emotionally with others through shared memories or shared feelings. It can make a person decide to help your cause, follow your leadership, or purchase your service or product. It can change mood, transcend place, and bridge time.

I recall seeing James Cameron's *Avatar* in 3D in an iMax theatre in Manhattan in December 2009. The movie theatre was packed with people, yet for over three hours strangers sat quietly transfixed. Parents, teens, fanboys, girls on dates, young children, older adults, blasé New Yorkers, and sci-fi movie lovers alike sat together in silence. We were riveted by the story and the special effects unfolding onscreen. We were rendered silent watching a unique film that was accompanied by an exquisite soundtrack by the indescribable James Horner (the soundtrack earned him an Oscar nomination, and he received the Max Steiner Award for Music in October 2013). Many of us will forever remember his haunting music, not just the movie's plot. Many of us can recall how the entire theatre was filled with cacophonous clapping and whistles at the end of the movie.

I have shared this experience with many people in my seminars, who also recall how almost everyone, in unison, surged to their feet and applauded at the end. Why? Would the actors or James Cameron know? Were they waiting in the wings, like on Broadway, to come out and take a bow? No, but we did it anyway. Why? Because we were all emotionally attuned to each other. We were strangers in sync with each other because we had all just shared a moment.

That's what emotional attunement is all about. It's the shared emotional reaction to the feelings of those around us and/or a re-action to an environmental trigger. Emotional attunement is like a sixth sense about what resonates with people. The best entrepreneurs either have this skill to begin with or hone it over time with practice. For interviews and sales pitches, cover letters and project proposals, as an effective entrepreneur you need to:

- Psych yourself up to complete your tasks and emote about your service or product and passionately inspire others to get on board your train.

- Gauge the emotional temperature of those in the room and try to establish a focal point, hopefully your pitch, which will emotionally resonate with the audience long after it's over.

How do you accomplish both? By channeling your inner musician and having a theme song playlist (yes, more than one song) for yourself, for your pitch, and for getting work done.

For those who remember the ground-breaking television show *Ally McBeal* (which I found to be funny, brilliant, and quite insightful about the human condition), you may recall that Ally (a rather neurotic but lovable lawyer played whimsically by Calista Flockhart) was told to have a theme song for herself. She was to sing or hum it before conducting trials in court and during difficult moments or periods in her life. Critics of the show lambasted Ally's rich inner life and her fantasy theme songs (remember the dancing baby?), which sometimes included entire productions and orchestras. Kind of like another later TV show that featured a male lawyer, Eli Stone, played with panache by Johnny Miller (which I also watched and enjoyed). In education we frequently tell children to "sing it to remember it," "sing away the blues," or "sing together to break the ice."

It's no wonder that music-themed television shows such as *American Idol, Glee,* and *The Voice* are very popular. It's no wonder that there are so many radio stations on the air. It's easier than ever to have your own inner anthem, even a playlist full of them for various occasions, thanks to the ever-growing popularity of the iPhone and iPod or built-in music players on other smartphones. There are also streaming, Internet-based music services like Pandora, Songza, Spotify, Rdio, and now Apple iRadio. I keep my SoundHound iOS App turned on in my iPhone whenever I'm driving my car. I never know when a song will come on the radio that will inspire me, which means that it should be added to my playlist for future reference when I'm working on or delivering a pitch.

I use these theme songs, these personal anthems, in different ways and at different times depending on my sales pitch, personal mood, and familiarity with my audience. My experiences in both education and on the lecture circuit have taught me to not underestimate the power of music. It can be used to promote a specific collective feeling, invoke a shared memory, or help me share a moment with my students, colleagues, and audiences. Try it and you'll see what I mean.

Penina's Pointers

Tips for Choosing Theme Songs Wisely

1. Make a list of catchy show tunes and television themes you remember fondly from childhood or from your iTunes library. You can also search Bing, Yahoo!, or Google online or visit this gem of a website, TelevisionTunes.com: http://bit.ly/TV-theme-songs.

2. Choose several tunes as possible personal theme songs. Your personal anthem should be a song with words that are meaningful to you, should help you remember a wonderful memory, and should have an upbeat tempo to actually get you moving and creative so you can commit to being in work mode as needed.

3. Create a digital folder somewhere (iTunes playlist, desktop computer, Dropbox, SugarSync, Amazon cloud drive, etc.) and name it Personal Anthem or Music for Meetings and store the MP3 files inside. As a safeguard, I recommend creating a folder inside your e-mail account and e-mailing yourself the files as a backup.

4. Create a playlist of catchy tunes, with lyrics appropriate for business settings and songs containing keywords you want for your actual pitch or slideshow. You can also use instrumental music as background or to evoke feelings and a specific response. I do it for most of my YouTube videos. Create a digital folder and back those up too.

5. Get a Google Alerts notification, in addition to doing a monthly search on your own, for new websites that compile databases of songs, genres, music clips, etc. Bookmark those sites for future reference, whether for yourself or for a future presentation.

6. Voila! You have just compiled the soundtrack to your life — your inner life, your work life, and, I hope, your inspired and inspiring life. You deserve an Oscar or a treat of your choice for your arrangement. Best of all, you can always change it and win one again.

The Power of Humor When Creating Your First Impression

KEY WEBSITES

- http://bit.ly/just-for-laughs-TV
- http://bit.ly/british-speaking-animals
- http://bit.ly/betty-white-off-their-rockers
- http://bit.ly/some-e-cards
- http://bit.ly/bil-keane-family-circus
- http://bit.ly/humorous-quotes
- http://bit.ly/facebook-funny-or-die
- http://bit.ly/facebook-amazing-weird
- http://bit.ly/pinterest-humor

Quotes to Ponder

Doing drama is, in a sense, easier. In doing comedy, if you don't get that laugh, there's something wrong.

— Betty White

Humor is mankind's greatest blessing.

— Mark Twain

Definition

Humor: The mental faculty of discovering, expressing, or appreciating the ludicrous or absurdly incongruous.

— *The Merriam-Webster Dictionary*

HUMOR IS A CHARACTERISTIC essential to the human experience and a crucial tool in the entrepreneur's arsenal. Humor helps you connect to others emotionally and feel included. Humor helps you cope and be resilient in the face of setbacks and challenges. Humor helps you internalize and retain memories and experiences, which shapes your perception and personality as you navigate the corridors of life. Humor develops in stages and, for this book, the two stages that I will refer to are physical and linguistic.

Physical humor prefaces human speech. In babies, physical humor emerges even before the first year, when a baby laughs at your funny faces or voices or sounds. It emerges initially as a physiological response, the release of endorphins — the feel-good hormones — in response to your body's reaction to something you see or hear. Physical humor, then, is essentially a human response to feedback from input received through your senses. It's a sentient response that involves the perception of incongruity — that something is out of place or off kilter. Since your life follows some semblance of order and routine, it's jarring when you sense an object in a "wrong" position. Slapstick humor, deadpan humor, and pantomime humor are all examples of physical humor. Mr. Bean (especially in the hilarious movie *Rat Race*), Abbott and Costello, Charlie Chaplin, Carol Burnett, Goldie Hawn, and other physical comedians all displayed this type of humor. The Debbie Downer character from *Saturday Night Live,* played by talented actress Rachel Dratch, first appeared in May 2004. She has forever immortalized and raised deadpan humor to an art form.

In the workplace today, where employees are hired and expected to work together like the Borg Cube from *Star Trek the Next Generation* (cogs in a well-oiled machine), physical humor is especially important to release tension and bring people together. When making this point in my seminars I usually like to show a 2010 Super Bowl ad about the Moose Head (http://bit.ly/monsterdotcom-moose).Why? Because it demonstrates how putting something in a weird position is so funny! The commercial shows a man who's been promoted and has a new office, complete with a moose head mounted on his wall for status (although in my book that's not really a status symbol, but maybe that's because I'm female and a city girl at that!). Unfortunately, on the other side of the wall, in the mail room, the poor guy, obviously in a cubicle, seems to have been ignored by the HR department. It's either an attempt to cut back on costs, or a slight for those lower on the totem pole, but the moose head hasn't been separated from the rest of its body. The back of the moose's body is mounted on *his wall*, causing obvious discomfort and difficulty! The result is an incongruous visual image for viewers to see and remember.

Whenever you start a presentation, sales pitch, business meeting, or group slideshow, it's important to break the ice with humor. But use physical humor wisely to initially share a moment (which we discussed earlier). Research has been done comparing the endorphin levels in people who had just experienced humor with those who had not. It was found that those people who experienced humor in groups were more likely to release endorphins (producing feelings of well-being). Think of all the TV commercials strategically placed at regular intervals during your favorite sitcom. Think of the Super Bowl ads each year, where there is actually a bidding war about product placement. Physical humor actually helps people bond emotionally. Physical humor can unite disparate viewpoints and create common ground *psychologically.*

It's linguistic humor, however, that creates common ground *intellectually.* It taps into your theory of mind or perspective. It creates a portal through which you access episodic memory. Linguistic humor thus helps you extrapolate from past events that are tied to vocabulary in your memory banks, so that you can bond over common language *and shared experiences.*

This is crucial when trying to bring others around to your way of thinking and to promote change through the proposals and meetings entrepreneurs engage in.

Linguistic humor is unique to human beings because it's tied to the seminal difference that sets us apart from other animals — speech. Linguistic humor is the culmination of your vocabulary development and comprehension of object function (language used to explain and retain information about how the world works). It's best used to create a first impression about you. The *you* that you're showing off when you're interviewing or presenting your pitch, product, or service. When you're on display, verbally and visually, in settings where everyone speaks the same language, dialect, and slang. Even if they're from different backgrounds, geographical locations, and/ or professions.

It's wise to keep in mind societal mores when using linguistic humor. It may be considered culturally rude, and even immature, to start with a joke using wording that's impolite, unfamiliar, or unprofessional. A good sense of humor is a sign of being in sync with your environment and those in it, especially in today's harried workplaces. Having a good sense of humor is a sign of being a self-aware, resilient, intelligent person. One who can learn from mistakes, take constructive criticism, and, best of all, lighten the collective mood. These are all important traits for an entrepreneur to have. Linguistic humor takes on various forms but always involves language of some sort as the punchline.

Here is a good example of linguistic humor — The Allstate Insurance commercial "Mayhem": http://bit.ly/allstate-mayhem.

Why is this funny? Because in 2013 when we hear a GPS chirp "recalculating" we access our episodic memory and know that either:

⊕ We're about to be sent into oncoming traffic

⊕ We're about to go down a one-way street towards a dead end

⊕ We're going to be so lost in a few minutes

The word *recalculating,* combined with our recall of what actually happened last time we heard that dreaded word, forms the episodic memory. The one that will be stored in the language center of your brain, the temporal lobe. It's housed there and brought out for later discussion during rueful laughter. But the word *recalculating* would have very different connotations for a sea captain, someone living in the era of Christopher Columbus, or for people working at the International Space Station. If a time traveler from even a hundred years ago would somehow see this commercial, would that confused person have a frame of reference that would allow them to see the humor?

Here's another example of linguistic humor: The Berlitz commercial, "Learn English Before It Is Too Late": http://bit.ly/berlitz-learn-english. This ad features linguistic humor centered around the word *expecting*. A man is in a corporate setting being interviewed by another man in English, which is seemingly not his native language. When asked what *he is expecting* from this job opportunity, the prospective employee responds along the lines of how his *wife* is the one *expecting*, and she is due soon.

Again, this commercial is funny, especially for women, because of the play on words. That's linguistic humor. That's why it can be a powerful business tool in your arsenal, *if* you know when to use it and to whom you are speaking.

In July 2013 a new Heineken ad got the attention of the marketing community, especially HubSpot. I commented on their 18 July 2013 blogpost (http://bit.ly/heineken-departure-roulette-review) that this isn't the first time Heineken has executed a brilliant marketing campaign.

But their new ad, "Departure Roulette," hits the ball out of the park because it targets a niche market, beer drinkers, within a larger culture, summer travelers. Also, it uses humor to help us tap into our collective episodic memories and cultural mores regarding when it's okay to break your word and deviate from the script of travel plans. This ad (http://bit.ly/heineken-departure-roulette) is a perfect example of the power of humor.

FAQ: What's The Difference Between Physical and Linguistic Humor?

- ✲ Physical humor relies on exaggerated or absurd facial affect or lack thereof (deadpan voice and/or expressions), causing people to pay extra attention to the words you say.

- ✲ Physical humor puts objects in unusual positions, causing the audience to pay extra attention and live in the moment to ponder the visual absurdity.

- ✲ Linguistic humor references concepts and nuances behind vocabulary words stored in episodic memory.

- ✲ Linguistic humor references the inner workings of your mind, not the outer workings of your body.

Penina's Pointers

Tips for Using Humor Wisely

1. Use funny but inoffensive pictures as an ice breaker and/or to make a point, keeping it short and sweet.

2. Use funny video clips as bookends for your interview, meeting, or pitch, and only if you were asked to bring a slideshow; otherwise tell a joke.

3. Use humor that's clean and not culturally insensitive — avoid roasts and scatological humor.

4. Use a photo or video clip of someone else, not you, doing something or saying something funny so that you don't become perceived as self-deprecating or the class clown.

5. Telling a joke or funny story that happened to you is okay in order to show commonalities, as long as you're not self-effacing or crude.

6. Use humor sparingly until you're more familiar with your audience so that you're perceived as serious about your purpose in that meeting or setting. Basically, make sure that when you do use humor, you use it wisely so you're well remembered.

Your Hook: Start with a Bang Using Video Clips

KEY WEBSITES

- http://bit.ly/youtube-home
- http://bit.ly/vimeo-home
- http://bit.ly/wimp-home
- http://bit.ly/hulu-home
- http://bit.ly/yahoo-screen-home
- http://bit.ly/online-video-guide

Quotes to Ponder

I'm a visual thinker.... My brain is like Google Images.

— Dr. Temple Grandin

All of life's riddles are answered in the movies.

— Steve Martin

Definition

Hook: Something intended to attract or ensnare. A selling point or marketing scheme.

— *The Merriam-Webster Dictionary*

ALL GOOD ENTREPRENEURS know the power of a first impression and the power of the hook. We know that your initial presentation on an interview, if you're asked to supply one, can make or break the interview. As a public speaker I've learned that the video footage I use in my digital slideshow can count more in hitting my point home than the words actually coming out of my mouth. I've also learned to often watch commercials instead of fast-forwarding through them on my DVR because I never know when I'll need fodder for one of my presentations or slideshows in order to make people laugh, bond, and relax.

I'm not going to give you advice on improving your public speaking skills. There are other books out there that can help with that. Besides, I hope you've already started to hone that skill. If not, get started. Watch TED speakers online, peruse Steve Jobs' videos of his keynote addresses and the famous graduation speech at Stanford, watch Greg Federighi's speech at the 2013 Apple Worldwide Developer's Conference, watch *Oprah,* even watch the Oscars for that matter.

I will, however, tell you later in this book how to create your hook more effectively using social media. There has never been a better time to increase the probability of your business plan's success through the use of technology, specifically by cross-pollinating social media to get your mission noticed. Keep in mind that it's essential to merge great public speaking capabilities with tech savvy to become a more vocally and digitally polished entrepreneur.

It pays to know a bit about the birth of the digital slideshow, which you'll use for your hook. The history of the digital, corporate slideshow began in 1990, when Microsoft PowerPoint made its debut alongside Windows 3.0 (PowerPoint was originally designed for the second wave of Macintosh computers released in 1987). The PowerPoint slideshow was developed by Dennis Austin and Thomas Rudkin as presenter slides that were linear, without the transitions we see today. PowerPoint was updated in 1997 to include more bells and whistles, which have since been renovated and perfected for today's presentation-software-centric workplace.

Today the term *PowerPoint* has become synonymous with the term *presentation.* However, many Apple users now prefer using the more sophisticated presentation software program Keynote, including me. PowerPoint slideshows were meant to be a brief, visual, informative way to boost work productivity and share information. But PowerPoint presentations have become a joke to many disgruntled employees — boring, uninformative, and a waste of time. Many bosses with poor public speaking skills but good technology skills unfortunately misuse PowerPoint.

A good slideshow is a clear example of substance over style. Yet people sometimes get bogged down in all the features offered by PowerPoint or Keynote. The digital presentation, then, becomes all about the cool transition, or the awesome font, instead of the message the speaker meant to convey. There are many comic strips poking fun at this cultural phenomenon, including one that features America's favorite cubicle-based employee, Dilbert (http://bit.ly/dilbert-on-powerpoint). This site showcases a collection of comic strips about PowerPoint and corporate meetings and presentations from Scott Adams, the creator of the beloved engineer Dilbert. Adams pokes fun at PowerPoint through references to business conduct, office politics, and data collection and demonstration (slides, pie charts, etc.). It's a funny, succinct analysis of the continuing struggle of substance vs. style in the office.

Good videos are also clear examples of substance and style. The history of the viral video began in 2005, when three young entrepreneurs, Steve Chen, Jawed Karim, and Chad Hurley, banded together to create the first behemoth, multimedia, user-generated video-sharing website for the masses — YouTube. In 2006 Google acquired YouTube, and the concept of social media integration really took off. YouTube became an overnight sensation. People could literally archive their episodic memory and dig into their visual and digital pasts for a collective show and tell. What a rush.

Old commercials, new movie trailers, snippets of music videos from MTV and CMT, and excerpts of shows from television now and then — it was all there on YouTube. Add to that the mixed-in family vacation and holiday videos, baby announcements, favorite pet moments, graduation speeches, and infomercials on how to do everything from knitting a scarf to decorating a cake like a pro. Later videos would include useful instructional tutorials and step-by-step procedural demonstrations for people learning about technology (how to make a ringtone on a smartphone), computers (how to create a backup of your hard drive), and education (how to build …). Some video offerings would remain inane, offensive, and unappealing reminders of the downside of democracy and freedom of speech. Anyone remember the gross parodies of *Sesame Street* or the Yahoo! polls on the most annoying videos? But all of them were available 24/7, on demand, and could be replayed, fast forwarded, or put on pause. How many of you have felt held hostage at work, or at a family gathering, being forced to view a slideshow until the end? Of course, thirty years ago families had a projector and hundreds of little slides to manually feed into the slot. Talk about a family reunion hostage situation.

YouTube really took off because of the sheer volume of possibilities and the potential for cross-pollination in terms of branding and marketing. Video clips could be marked as favorites, categorized, bookmarked, and shared. People could create their own space — a virtual portfolio on YouTube — and personalize it. We made a channel ours by uploading our own video content, streaming another person's suggestions, and making use of tags. I invite you to view my own digital kaleidoscope on YouTube, socialslp (http://bit.ly/socialslp). I invite you to create your own.

The implications of YouTube have been far-reaching. People in education, technology, healthcare, and business are all competing for airtime, not to mention that all-powerful music clip that will stay in people's consciousness. Social media evangelists, bloggers, marketing gurus, entrepreneurs, students, and parents of children with autism and other special needs have all gotten on board. We flock to make sense of this new frontier and to carve a space for ourselves in a YouTube universe that almost seems sentient.

Having lived in the late 80s in the aftermath of the birth of the personal computer, which heralded the beginning of the first leg of the Tech Revolution that started in the 90s (our introduction to cyberspace and e-mail), I was intrigued from the start. I watched the initial goings-on at YouTube carefully, and anonymously, until I launched my own company, Socially Speaking™ LLC, in 2010. Then I stepped out onto the digital stage to share my message.

YouTube is a tool that can be wielded for good. It can facilitate the effective marketing you need to provide as an entrepreneur. It can lead to a positive outcome, the change that you hope your legacy, your service, your product, will bestow upon the world.

On 4 June 2012, *Forbes* magazine ran an article by Rahim Kanani entitled, "Why YouTube is the Ultimate Platform for Global Social Change" (http://bit.ly/youtube-and-social-change). The director of product management at YouTube, Hunter Walk, was interviewed, and he discussed the positive implications for philanthropy, entrepreneurship, education, environmentalism, and social causes. He explained his vision for YouTube to become a shared, "more social, fulfilling, and open platform." Walk highlighted the changes in the social media landscape and the demographic shifts in viewer interests and activism. He even provided a valuable tip for users creating meaningful content on their own channels, especially if they want to implement change and social reform. "Nonprofits trying to use YouTube should remember three c's: *content, community, and call-to-action.*"

One of the first steps to take to become a bona fide entrepreneur is to create your hook and publicize it using YouTube and other social media. To create a digital footprint with a video that simply yet eloquently tells others what you're about. I recommend that female entrepreneurs, concerned about road travel due to physical safety risks as well as the difficulty of maintaining their home front, take note and create a free YouTube channel. You have a particular stake in this. I suggest that you take advantage of the free social media and video-sharing sites such as YouTube, Vimeo, Facebook, Google+, Pinterest, About.Me, Tumblr, and Twitter and establish an online presence where you can:

- ⚙ Share music and video clips of your mission statement, services or products, or how you can help fix problems.

- ⚙ Share links to others who seem to share your vision and aspirations.

- ⚙ Impart small doses of news-you-can-use-style posts, where you provide information about the industry you're currently in or trying to get into and what's trending in that particular ecosystem.

You don't have to become a slave to your social media sites. There is software, such as those created by HubSpot and HootSuite, that can help you get control of your social media activities. Their webinars, blogs, free e-books, and social media sites are fountains of information. There are websites that can help you with content curation, which is becoming a viable, profitable marketing strategy, such as Alltop.com, Slate.com, Digg.com, as well as specific apps (I adore Zite). Find out which playground your demographic frequents, and make that your focal point. Get into the habit of posting meaningful content every other day or so, more if you actually have something important to say about an event or if you were specifically asked to repost something. It's okay to post on YouTube more sparingly, but make those uploads count. Also make sure to visit YouTube regularly, albeit anonymously. You know you do it, too! Just remember to sometimes sign in so that you can tag videos. That way you stay current and find videos that will inspire you when you create your own.

Another reason I encourage you to create a video channel for your arsenal is to leave a trail (in a favorites list if you want to be more organized) of video content that you want to save in order to:

- ❀ Emulate and recreate at your own meetings

- ❀ Keep track of the various pitches and mission statement slideshows you've created

- ❀ Use in future presentations and meetings

I've been asked in interviews for a timeline of my activities, and I find it to be easy and painless to provide an e-mail link with specific videos on my channel about where and when I've given specific seminars. I gave educational technology seminars right after the 2013 Super Bowl where I went online mid-sentence and used a video to hit home my point about the iPad's interface being user-friendly (because it puts everything front and center). Here's the "Hyundai Turbo-Stuck" ad I showed: http://bit.ly/hyundai-ad-stuck.

This commercial features a couple driving in a Hyundai car with an accelerator (turbo-boost) button. The husband uses it when he finds himself behind a truck apparently carrying nuclear warheads, which he understandably wants to move ahead of. He also uses it when behind a trailer with slobbering dogs whose heads are hanging out the window creating projectile missiles of saliva onto the Hyundai's windshield. These are just two of the hilarious scenarios depicted. The message? "It's just better to be in front." My message in my seminars as an iPad evangelist is the same — the iPad, which literally puts everything at your fingertips, puts you in front! That's why I love this ad so much.

Don't have WiFi access in the middle of your pitch or seminar? This is becoming a growing concern, and the blogger Maggie Mc-Gary commented on it recently when she wrote about the issues with cost, privacy, and bandwidth that conference attendees face when networking at hotels and attending business functions and events. It seems that Facebook will soon offer WiFi service that allows speakers to offer their audiences free WiFi after they check in on the social network (http://bit.ly/free-wifi-from-facebook).

Figure 2-1. People are visual creatures. They often use visual clues to understand their environment.

I've been dealing with this issue for a long time by uploading You-Tube videos to my Keynote slideshow before my presentation using a free extension for the Firefox Internet browser on my desktop computer only. You can download the extension here: http://bit.ly/capture-videos-in-firefox.

People are visual creatures. How do you know where the rest-room is when you're in a hotel in a foreign country? How do you know that the hotel means business and you will incur a hefty fine, not to mention the wrath of the manager, if you fail to heed their visual warnings? (See Figure 2 1.)

The power of visuals is why I always use short, often funny, video clips as bookends to my presentation as well as before and after breaks. I want to offer my audience food for thought to increase camaraderie and, yes, emotional attunement so that those in attendance are receptive to my hook.

There's another benefit to using videos in marketing your hook, as seen from Twitter's recent launch of Vine for Instagram. Unlike You-Tube, Vine videos have a six-second limitation, providing an instant sales pitch for busy people at work or on break, or people with short attention spans growing ever shorter with increasingly long lists of available distractions out there. Furthermore, the very architecture of Vine showcases the need for mobile-based marketing for the public's growing appetite to market, share, and digest meaningful and even banal content on the go, using mobile devices (http://bit.ly/marketing-to-short-attention-spans).

Visual digitalization marketing — the use of a visual image, sometimes accompanied by a phrase, to convey an entire message — is the driving force behind new trends in social media. But at the end of the day it's finding the absurd in the human condition and sharing a moment by collectively laughing about it that spurs collective change, promotes content marketing, and gives the competitive, solitary, sometimes grueling nature of entrepreneurship its wings to be free and brings it more in touch with humanity.

Penina's Pointers

Tips for Using Videos for Your Hook

1. Create a YouTube channel and even a Vimeo channel (depends what industry you're in) as a holding pen for video clips that catch your eye as both an entrepreneur and a consumer. Tag funny videos that can help you humorously create your hook, and add steadily to your favorites list for future reference.

2. Upload self-created video content for marketing, content about your mission statement and your service or product and timeline. Your content will be handy for later use in various meetings, pitches, or interviews in both physical space and cyberspace.

3. Download video clips directly into your digital slideshow, if you can, using the two websites I listed above for those times when you don't have a WiFi connection and don't want to lose momentum while giving your hook.

4. Use video content wisely for your hook, at meaningful intervals, so that you have a *receptive* audience, not a captive audience.

iOS Apps for Presentations:
User-Friendly Slideshows

KEY WEBSITES

- http://bit.ly/keynote-for-ipad
- http://bit.ly/free-ipad-presentation-apps
- http://bit.ly/ipad-presentation-apps
- http://bit.ly/haiku-deck-for-presentations
- http://bit.ly/slideshark-app-for-powerpoints
- http://bit.ly/prezi-for-presentations
- http://bit.ly/powtoon-animated-videos
- http://bit.ly/doceri-whiteboard
- http://bit.ly/google-drive-file-storage
- http://bit.ly/freemind-mind-mapping
- http://bit.ly/mindmeister-mind-mapping
- http://bit.ly/pixplit-photo-collage-app
- http://bit.ly/make-your-message-stick

Quotes to Ponder

It's interesting to talk about ... something you're doing for somebody else, and particularly if you can persuade others to join you....

— Wendie Malick

All the forces in the world are not so powerful as an idea whose time has come.

— Victor Hugo

Definition

Presentation: the manner or style in which something is given, offered, or displayed.

— New Oxford American Dictionary

SAY THE WORD *presentation* today and it brings to mind all sorts of images of tech gadgets. Any entrepreneur will tell you that the purpose of a presentation is to provide an idea that will educate, entertain, persuade, and generate responses. The purpose of a slideshow, one of the most popular presentation forms used today, is to *visually* inform and motivate others about your agenda, purpose, and desired outcomes, short term and long term. A good presenter actively inspires the audience. A great presenter helps the audience members tap into their collective memory banks (episodic memory) using words, images, messages, and ideas that will foster emotional attunement and creativity. You need to be a good (or better yet, great) presenter to be a successful entrepreneur.

In *Good to Great,* author Jim Collins writes, "When used right, technology becomes an accelerator of momentum, not a creator of it. The good-to-great companies never began their transitions with pioneering technology, for the simple reason that you cannot make good use of technology until you know which technologies are relevant." This was written in 2001, years before the tech boom and social media movement.

It's well known that today's entrepreneur needs to keep up with mobile technology trends, particularly apps, simply because presentation apps are evolving and becoming powerful tools for your virtual toolbox. Many of us were taught PowerPoint, the first software program to be integrated into school-wide curriculums across the United States. Adults in the past two decades usually learned it in college, on the fly at work, or from their own children learning it in school. Given the omnipresence of PowerPoint, nobody could have predicted that one day many people, including me, would easily and happily replace it with a more portable presentation app.

Today's entrepreneur needs to adapt to the increasingly popular tablet presentation tools and learn about the various ways to present a slideshow on a mobile device, especially an iPad. I am vocally, unabashedly, and unconditionally a Mac user; have been since I was a child. My friends and family know this, and thanks to my social media sites and seminars, people near and far now know about my love for all things Apple. Now you will too.

I believe that the iPad is a tremendous game changer in the worlds of business and education, particularly special education. That's where I was introduced to educational technology, using Apple software and products, and that's where I unofficially got my start as an entrepreneur. I participated in the 1995–2000 New York State TRAID Project (Technology Related Assistance for Individuals with Disabilities), piloted by the Westchester Institute for Human Development. I was one of the first ones in New York state to be trained by what would later become the Apple Educators Program. So Apple and I go way back, and integrating Apple tech into my presentations and lesson plans (and now books) has become instinctive.

It's beyond the scope of this book, however, to write about the various tablets and mobile devices and the slideshow, presentation, and meeting apps available for entrepreneurs today. A good search engine will provide you with a plethora of information, as will the reputable tech blogs. I stay in the technology loop thanks to social media sites and the customization feature of my favorite digital magazine app for my iPad, Zite. It's my most valuable app to use when trying to stay current. Zite lets me customize my reading experience and learns what I want to know about. The more I use it the more it learns about me and the more it helps me focus on retrieving and storing the information that is truly essential for me to know.

Customization is the key word for what makes any app great and what separates a successful entrepreneur from a struggling one. As a successful entrepreneur you'll use insight gained about multiple intelligences, humor, mobile technology, and habits and haunts of your target audience to customize and deploy your hook — to create slideshows and perform theatrically while presenting them. Good presentations are based on slideshows with meaningful and relevant content, creativity, calculated imagery, and some mild coercion.

Take this example from the popular TV show on Bravo, *Million Dollar Listing*. I caught the 3 May 2013 episode on a JetBlue flight, trying to distract my queasy stomach from reacting to the severe turbulence. This real estate reality show featured a home (actually a huge apartment) on the market. It was decided that the showing would include a staging of live people modeling different poses in the various rooms. It seemed that Ryan, the host, felt that the prospective buyers needed to see more than just a static apartment, and that the architecture and furniture were not enough of a backdrop or a framework for the message he wanted to convey. I'd never seen this show, but I took notes on it (using the Notes app from my iPad, of course) to remember for this book. Another item added to my Good Ideas to Try list, namely customize your presentation.

A tech gadget's greatest selling point is its customization feature. It resides within each app, in terms of the hardware and user interface, which you customize by tweaking the settings button on the control panel. It also resides in each app's toolbar, which can often be tweaked by the individual user at any time. This allows for better integration of the hardware and software portions of the mobile device. You should thus get into the habit of customizing the device's settings and the app's toolbar when creating or displaying a slideshow.

Any project, especially a good presentation, is the sum of its parts. Artists know this. Entrepreneurs know this. Steve Jobs knew this. And so does Apple CEO Tim Cook. He reportedly fired the initial designer of the iOS architecture, Scott Forstall, because he wasn't enough of a team player and seemed uninterested in collaborating and sharing information and ideas. That really resonated with me, as someone who learned the value of collaboration early on, as a woman, and as a pediatric, school-based speech therapist working with a team.

At the end of May 2013, at the *Wall Street Journal*'s All Things Digital (D11) Conference in California, Tim Cook discussed how popular the iPad is. He reported that the iPad has one of the most consistently high satisfaction ratings among consumers and that it's projected to become a top-selling product. There's ongoing speculation that sales have skyrocketed in two sectors: education and small business. The Apple App Store is furiously churning out new apps. Our collective appetite for new tech and new apps is by no means diminishing. Entrepreneurs and tech-savvy individuals are banding together to attempt to balance the supply and demand seesaw. The seesaw that capitalism is built on.

As both a professional speaker and an iPad app creator, I'm very aware of the challenges of the available iPad real estate in terms of layout (portrait-mode viewing vs. landscape-mode viewing). Layout is of concern when doing a presentation for a live audience, whether in an office meeting or a hotel conference room.

Why use an iPad for your presentation or slideshow? I've learned that doing a slideshow with an iPad app is the difference between serving a lone brownie on a plate or serving a long-stemmed glass filled with miniature brownie chunks, chocolate mousse, chocolate sauce, ice cream, and caramelized nuts and whipped cream. You decide.

Visually pleasing slideshows will linger longer in the mind's eye. Technically pleasing slideshows, whose simplicity appeals to today's multitasking entrepreneur, will facilitate longer presentations. Just remember that less is more — don't create unnecessary slides. Create work that matters. For more on that subject, I refer you to the excellent book from the creators of the company 37signals, *Rework*, specifically pages 100–2. I use their to-do list of questions to ponder when creating presentations for project proposals embedded in my pitches:

1. Why are you doing this?

2. What problem are you solving?

3. Is this actually useful?

4. Are you adding value?

5. Will this change behavior?

6. Is there an easier way?

7. What could you be doing instead?

8. Is it really worth it?

When asked about which visually pleasing, relatively simple-to-use, inexpensive (some are free), and iOS-friendly presentation apps are on my radar, I usually supply a specific list, in a specific order. See my list at the end of this chapter.

When asked about ways to organize content for the slideshow (the script), I refer people to the varied writings of the ubiquitous, knowledgeable, easy-to-read, first Apple evangelist, most famous Google+ proponent, and all-around interesting Guy Kawasaki. In his ground-breaking books *Selling the Dream* and *The Art of the Start* he succinctly gives us concrete guidelines to follow when implementing a presentation. I have not always followed them, much to my chagrin and detriment, which is why I am diligently including them in this book. There are basically five guidelines to follow:

- ⚙ Stress empowerment to inspire others to join you

- ⚙ Communicate your ambition and most crucial goals

- ⚙ Highlight their personal benefit(s), to enhance relevance

- ⚙ Reach an emotional peak midway, to excite the audience

- ⚙ Follow the 10/20/30 rule: Use 10 slides in your presentation, speak for 20 minutes, and don't use fonts smaller than 30 points

Penina's Pointers

Tips for Using Presentation Apps

1. Make sure you cover the 3 Es: educate, entertain, and encourage change.

2. Be organized about the visual content for your slides. Keep a folder (either on your desktop or camera's SD card — yes, you can use it like a thumb drive) of inspirational photos that you took yourself (preferred method, less of an issue with copyright infringement) or found online in Google Images to use again and again as needed (remember to use license-free photos). These links can help:

    ⊕ http://bit.ly/google-image-search

    ⊕ http://bit.ly/find-license-free-images

3. Even if you're a dyed-in-the-wool PC user or Android apps lover, consider purchasing an iPad (with a business credit card, of course) that you'll start off using for presentations, and watch yourself start to use it for other things.

4. Create a famous-quotes holding pen using a word processing document or note (e-mail it to yourself and/or save it in Google Drive, Dropbox, Amazon Cloud, or another cyber-closet) where you list your favorite, relevant, and inspirational quotes to use in either your slideshow, handout, or both. Never underestimate the power of a one-liner or great quote to kick off the presentation. You can find online quotes here:

- http://bit.ly/quotation-search
- http://bit.ly/brainy-quote
- http://bit.ly/thinkexist-quotations

5. Remember to use humor (quotes, photos, comics, video clips) as bookends to your slideshow. Keep in mind the human factor, too — it's not just about the technology.

6. Don't get bogged down in the transitions of each slide (the visual effects going from one slide to the next, like fades or dissolves). Don't lose momentum, become busy with your remote, or distract your audience from the message you're trying to convey. Wow them with the content of your slideshow, not just your technical prowess.

7. Learn about various visual modalities available today for the tech-savvy entrepreneur. You may have greater impact using a slideshow made of sequential slides, but sometimes a digital poster, or a mind map (flow chart) of the trajectory of your project is warranted. Sometimes a single infographic speaks volumes. Look at the new Google Dashboard for templates. As you become more knowledgeable about the different iOS apps, software programs, online services, and tech gadgets available, you can make more informed choices of which one best fits your needs in that moment (see my examples, Figures 2-2 to 2-5, on the following pages).

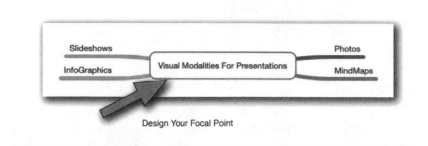

Figure 2-2. Sample mind map. Image created by Penina using the MindNode app for the iPad.

FAQ: What's an Infographic?

A N INFOGRAPHIC is a visual presentation, usually digital, of data, information, or knowledge that's often difficult to understand quickly. It's used as a learning and marketing tool because the information is easy to scan and understand. Why are infographics so popular? Because we're visual creatures, with limited time, living in a globally connected reality where we need to engage in quick, universally understood communication that will stick. I learned the value of infographics during my work with students with autism, who are predominantly visual learners. In 2012 the rest of the world caught on as social media and mobile devices became more prevalent in people's toolboxes. Here are some important links with more information on infographics:

- http://bit.ly/why-infographics-work
- http://bit.ly/create-infographics-online
- http://bit.ly/infographics-archive
- http://bit.ly/free-infographics-tools
- http://bit.ly/slideshare-infographics-player
- http://bit.ly/hubspot-on-slideshare-infographics
- http://bit.ly/infographics-in-excel

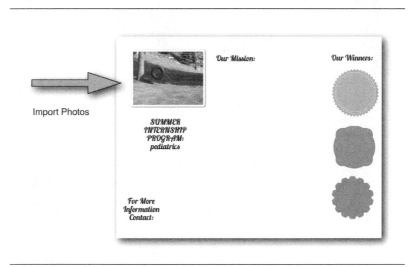

Figure 2-3. Sample digital poster. Image created by Penina using the Grafio app for the iPad.

iOS Apps for Entrepreneurial Presentations — Penina's Picks

Infographic Apps

- ⊛ Grafio ($; lite version doesn't work with a projector, but the customizable photo import feature rocks)

- ⊛ MindMeister (free; great mind-mapping and flow-charting features for discussing a sequence of events or outcomes)

- ⊛ Popplet ($; educators love this one — great for quick meetings)

- ⊛ Notability ($; known as a PDF editor app, too)

Presentation Apps

- Keynote (free; Apple's checkmate to PowerPoint, and my favorite)
- Haiku Deck (free; can import Google Images)
- Prezi (free)
- SlideShark (free; works with already-made PowerPoint slides)
- ShowMe (free)
- ScreenChomp (free; educators and students love this one)
- Educreations (free; educators can form communities and share slideshows)
- Doceri (free)
- Explain Everything ($)
- Final Argument ($)

iPad Mirroring Apps

- Reflector ($)
- AirServer ($)
- AirParrot ($)
- iTools ($)

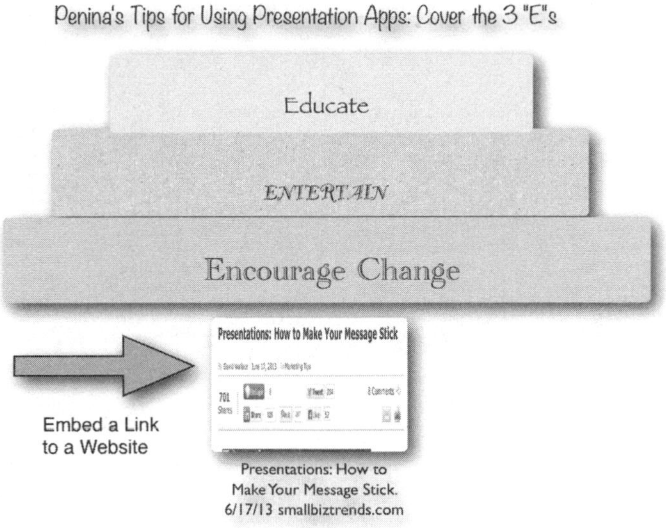

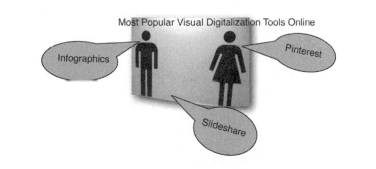

Figure 2-4. Sample basic infographic. Image created by Penina using the Notability app for the iPad.

Figure 2-5. Sample basic infographic. Image created by Penina using Apple's Pages for iOS app.

THREE

Upgrading Your Tech IQ
with an iPad

C = COMPETENT

The Importance of iOS Apps

KEY WEBSITES

- http://bit.ly/macworld-ios-apps-news
- http://bit.ly/mashable-best-free-ipad-apps
- http://bit.ly/digital-trends-best-ipad-apps
- http://bit.ly/tech-support-alert-free-ipad-apps
- http://bit.ly/ipad-insight
- http://bit.ly/ipad-learning-in-hand
- http://bit.ly/education-tech
- http://bit.ly/apps-to-save-you-money
- http://bit.ly/ios7-tips-and-tricks
- http://bit.ly/90-ios7-tips-and-tricks
- http://bit.ly/best-things-about-ios7

- ⌐ http://bit.ly/hidden-ios7-features
- ⌐ http://bit.ly/ios7-how-to-guide
- ⌐ http://bit.ly/best-ipad-tips-and-tricks
- ⌐ http://bit.ly/tricks-for-ipad-users
- ⌐ http://bit.ly/ipad-mini-tips-and-tricks

Quotes to Ponder

When people think about computer science, they imagine people with pocket protectors and thick glasses who code all night.

— Marissa Mayer

Genius is one percent inspiration and ninety nine percent perspiration.

— Thomas Edison

Definition

App, application: A piece of software designed and written to fulfill a particular purpose of the user.

— *New Oxford American Dictionary*

Ask a child today where to buy an app, and you'll likely hear the casual response, "the App Store, of course." App, short for the word *application,* has become part of our daily vernacular and part of our daily routines, making our mobile devices virtually indispensable. Whether your smartphone or tablet runs on the iOS platform (Apple) or the Android one, the phrase "there's an app for that" has never been more true.

Apple launched the App Store as part of iTunes in July 2008. There were only 500 apps to sell at that time. Three months later, the Android Market (now Google Play) was launched for people in the PC world, for Windows users clamoring for their fair share. There were only 50 apps to sell them initially. As time passed, app developers from both stores joined the startup culture, reinventing the rules and the roles for what it means to be an entrepreneur in our technology-driven society.

The 2010 debut of the iPad forever altered the linear trajectory of the advancement of app integration into our zeitgeist and into mainstream culture. Today app stores (for both iOS and Android) resemble the Wild West just a bit. Many apps today are products of creativity, functionality, productivity, undercutting prices, and marketing attempts. That's why there are free, paid, discounted, and holiday-themed versions of prototypes. Their success is determined by the fast-paced roller coaster ride in which they are unveiled, hawked, and finally purchased by the consumer. And if the consumer isn't tech savvy to begin with, the entire process becomes more confusing and frustrating. Especially for female entrepreneurs with little experience with technology, let alone iOS apps. What's a girl to do?

STEM courses (science, technology, engineering, math) have always been considered the last bastions of the educational version of an "all boys club." Research has shown this to be true and continues to be done on this topic (more on this later). In April 2012 the journal *Gender and Society* published a disturbing article (http://bit. ly/females-lag-behind-in-math; http://bit.ly/math-teacher-bias). An article about a University of Texas study at an Austin high school conducted by Dr. Catherine Riegle-Crumb and her doctoral student, Melissa Humphries.

The study revealed an unconscious, small-but-noticeable bias by math teachers against white female students in the teachers' perceptions and scoring of the students' work. "If the math bias against females is present in elementary school, which past research shows it is, and continues through high school and then college, then it's much less likely that you will find women pursuing math-related, high-status occupations in science and technology," said Riegle-Crumb. This study garnered national attention from various sources, including the authors of *Freakonomics*, Steven Levitt and Stephen Dubner.

The Freakonomics Duo have had their hands full since broadcasting their February 2013 podcast "Women Are Not Men" (http://bit.ly/women-are-not-men). They questioned the validity of the nature vs. nurture debate surrounding gender roles and expectations around the world but especially in the Western World. They interviewed people who highlighted differences between men and women in various business arenas including patents (men file more), research and development in corporations (men engage in development and design more), social media (women are more active participants but tend to follow rather than provide thought leadership), philanthropy (men are less likely to do someone a favor according to Dubner) and publishing and editing (women are on the rise albeit slowly).

The podcast also garnered attention from its discussion about women being more sanitary (men wash their hands less often according to Dubner), being more apt to admit to not knowing something, and having less leisure time than men. It was also pointed out that men these days are having more life satisfaction and tolerance for conflict than women, which plays a role in work/life balance and office politics, particularly regarding collaboration on time-sensitive projects.

Uri Gneezy, a behavioral economist from the Rady School of Management at the University of California, San Diego, was interviewed and recalled that when raising his two girls and boy, he "really tried to raise them in a gender-neutral environment." Yet he realized that gender did affect the quality of their play schemas with dolls and trucks, even though they happily played with both. He gave his explanation for the continuing gender gap. "An important difference is how willing men and women are to compete and how they react to competitive incentives. Culture [nurture] is so big, can be so big, it can just overturn results [one's nature]."

The overall consensus around the water cooler and blogosphere is that the gender gap appears to be closing somewhat but differences persist. These differences are evident in the way women approach technology, competition, personal happiness, and job satisfaction. Ask a female entrepreneur about these crucial but rarely discussed factors. Ask women in the workplace about their performance in these areas. You'll get some surprisingly uncomfortable answers and impressions. The Great Divide does indeed still exist.

Implications for Entrepreneurs

GOOD ENTREPRENEURS know how to wear the actor hat and the tech support hat when giving their hook. Today's successful entrepreneurs need to use both technology and intuition to create a presentation that really packs a punch. Yet so many women still think of themselves as *technophobes* today, slow to embrace new gadgets and apps. Apps that can actually help us move forward in closing some of the gender gap and opening new dialogues, especially in the workplace.

A disquieting blog post appeared in May 2013 (http://bit.ly/wwdc-and-women), a month before the Apple Worldwide Developer's Conference (WWDC) in San Francisco. The anonymous male blogger lamented the fact that he had to wait in line to go to the restroom at the last conference he attended, but that the women's restroom was essentially unused. While he humorously quipped how he always assumed a "que at the loo" was a female invention, the ramifications of there being very few female app developers in attendance at the WWDC did not go unnoticed at the event or in this article. The male blogger went on to implore Apple to follow in the footsteps of another prominent company, Etsy. This company was proactive in addressing the paucity of female app developers and established a full scholarship training program over the summer in San Francisco. The program was a huge success, and many women opted to stay and work for Etsy after the summer was over. Yet too few women attend one of the biggest tech events of the year, the WWDC. Too few women embrace app development, let alone app integration into the creative process of giving a presentation or into the workflow of a daily project. I was so bothered by this article that I ended up writing an e-mail to Tim Cook, CEO of Apple, and posting it as an Open Letter to Tim Cook on my Facebook and Google+ pages, Socially Speaking™ LLC. You can still find it there and on my Slideshare page as well. I was bothered because the reality this gentleman saw in San Francisco is similar to the reality I see in my travels and lectures.

I just spent an interesting, exhilarating, informative, and very educational two years on the road in North America. This past year was spent traveling roughly two weeks each month giving a variety of professional seminars, including one about educational technology. In that very specialized seminar, iPad Basics and iOS App Integration, I learned a lot behind closed doors about what's really trending for working women. I asked questions, conducted informal surveys, kept notes, and found patterns. Patterns of human behavior shaped by the uneasy marriage between gadgets and "girl-chores," as the boys used to call them when we were young.

I found that geographical location played a huge role in the level of accessibility and familiarity the members of my informal focus group had with iPad apps. I learned that location — whether in the United States (West Coast, Midwest, South, or Northeast) or in Canada — pre-determined the gender, socio-economic status, and level of technophobia of my audiences. I also found a disquieting trend among many attendees who were 30- and 40-something female professionals in the healthcare and educational sectors. Many appeared exhausted. They talked of juggling family, work, keeping house, attempts at personal growth, and community responsibilities with an ever-changing, ever-increasing learning curve with regard to technology. Some women confided that because new apps are constantly coming out of the woodwork, using technology has become a dreaded chore. Some lamented that their children knew more than they did. Some women had been given carte blanche to purchase iOS apps for work but simply couldn't be motivated, find the time, or figure out how.

I must point out: not all the wonderful, educated, devoted, and creative women I encountered displayed sensory overload or ennui. Many women in my audiences of various ages and backgrounds embraced the technology and taught us a few tricks to implement immediately. I got a good laugh and hearty agreement from many of these praiseworthy, hardworking, and determined women when I quoted Jane Austen's famous line from *Pride and Prejudice* when, while seated at the piano, Elizabeth Bennett tells Mr. Darcy: "Perhaps you should take your aunt's advice and practice?"

Many have since kept in touch with me, via my social media sites or e-mail, letting me know how much they are trying and practicing and how much better they are now at integrating apps into their work projects. I've increasingly gotten requests to mentor other female entrepreneurs and share what I've learned. I've realized that there are a few concrete tips I would like to impart. Let me attempt "to make the medicine go down" more easily (as another literary icon, the ever-wise and popular Mary Poppins, would say). For those of you unfamiliar with technology, here are my tips.

Penina's Pointers

Tips for Integrating iOS Apps into Painless Presentations

1. Set some time aside at least once a week. Do online searches and learn about the features of various apps available for your mobile device. Play around with a few apps while commuting, waiting in the car (not while driving!), or watching TV. *Make mistakes!* Wow yourself first and then others with a short, really cool, multimedia, interactive performance, such as a slideshow using the Photos App or a slideshow app such as Keynote. (Note: I'm often asked how hard it is to learn Keynote, a paid app for iOS devices. In my opinion, it blows PowerPoint, also a paid app, right out of the water. Keynote, being truly multisensory, methodical, and customizable, is actually a lot of fun to learn, and the possibilities are almost endless. But don't take my word for it. Try it out for free and see what I mean.)

2. There are several great free presentation/slideshow apps that are iOS and Android compatible such as Prezi, Slideshark, Powtoon, and Google Drive Slides. For an iOS device you can't beat the ones listed at the end of the previous chapter. You can read descriptions of them in iTunes, see demos on YouTube, or visit the app websites to see showcases of what others have done (check out Haiku Deck in particular).

3. If you want more information, there are reputable tech blogs online, with a multitude of tips and tricks.

Websites of the *The New York Times, The Wall Street Journal, The Huffington Post, Macworld, Cult of Mac, Mashable, Lifehacker, CNET, TechCrunch,* and *The Next Web* are filled with helpful articles (http://bit.ly/social-media-and-tech-blogs).

4. You know the expression "the family that plays together stays together"? Find time for other family members who may be more tech-savvy to sit with you and do a show and tell. Pick an app and, taking notes, have that person walk you through some of the app's finer points. You'll share a moment and actually learn something useful.

For the remainder of this chapter, which will read somewhat like a cookbook, you'll be introduced to my recommended secret weapon for entrepreneurs — the game-changing iPad. I re-created some of the content below from my 2012 and 2013 Socially Speaking™ iPad Basics Bootcamp Seminars for this crash course on iPad jargon and its uses for busy entrepreneurs. This should be especially useful for those of you who are unfamiliar with the world of Apple and iOS. So grab your iPad, and grab your highlighter. Get ready, get set, go!

iPad Basics: Where to Start

KEY WEBSITES

- http://bit.ly/ipad-user-guide
- http://bit.ly/ipad-essentials
- http://bit.ly/telegraph-guide-to-the-ipad
- http://bit.ly/secrets-for-ipad
- http://bit.ly/free-guide-to-your-ipad
- http://bit.ly/guide-to-ios7
- http://bit.ly/master-ios7
- http://bit.ly/use-evernote-on-your-tablet
- http://bit.ly/iwork-for-icloud
- http://bit.ly/ios7-keyboard-shortcuts
- http://bit.ly/complete-guide-to-ios7
- http://bit.ly/ios-guides

Quotes to Ponder

When you're a dancer, you start with the basics. You don't all of a sudden do a grand jete and pirouette.

— Rita Rudner

Design is a funny word. Some people think design means how it looks. But of course, if you dig deeper, it's really how it works.

— Steve Jobs

Definition

THE WORD *iPad* is not yet an entry in many dictionaries, but if you search online you'll come across one entry from pcmag.com's Encyclopedia. It defines the iPad as "... a tablet computer from Apple ... designed for Web browsing, e-mail, e-book reading, and entertainment." I define it as the secret workhorse weapon of choice for future entrepreneurs. I say that because of its many benefits, which include: intuitive touch-screen technology, seamless integration of apps, app features, app data-sharing possibilities, sustainability, and overall portability. When the iPad was unveiled by Steve Jobs in 2010, *The Wall Street Journal* wrote, "Last time there was this much excitement about a tablet, it had some commandments written on it." So let's learn more about this innovative tech gadget that so many love to use at work and at home. When asked why I recommend this particular mobile device to other entrepreneurs, established or just starting out, I answer as follows: It helps you to become a more competent entrepreneur.

The iPad is an intuitive, creative, visually appealing mobile technology device. It promotes multitasking, which is crucial for us women in our daily balancing acts. It promotes sustainability (going green), which is crucial for us women to consider as part of our legacy for future generations. I often joke that the difference between using this particular platform in business today, as opposed to what was available a decade ago, is like the difference between writing with a pencil and a Montblanc pen. The difference is about quality, efficiency, and time management.

Penina's Pointers

The Top 10: What You Should Know About the iPad

1. It can be a stand-alone device or synced to a computer's iTunes library for home sharing of music, movies, photos, contacts, and calendar events, or to Dropbox, Google Drive, Amazon Cloud, or Sugar Sync for easy file sharing and transfer. The iOS 7 feature Airdrop is a nice addition to the iPad's functionality.

2. It contains a tracer to prevent theft (Settings > iCloud > Find My iPad > ON).

3. It uses Gestures such as finger-swiping for easier navigation.

4. It has the ability to categorize apps into folders for a customized user interface.

5. It can stream *all* your e-mail accounts' content to one location for easy viewing.

6. It can access printers wirelessly and print directly from many native and non-native apps; or you can export data as a photo or PDF.

7. You can dictate speech to text for apps such as E-mail, Notes, and Pages, using the microphone in the keyboard.

8. It contains a very fast browser, Safari, *native* to Apple, which allows you to:

    ❀ Turn on private browsing and clear your history (Settings > Safari > Clear History) as needed.

⊛ Use the Reader option to read the content you're browsing later (Add to Reading List) or use Pocket or Evernote to create your own, free, digital portfolio (holding pen).

⊛ Configure Bookmarks, Add Site to Bookmarks, or Add Site to Home Screen as needed.

⊛ E-mail the page or link of the website you're interested in for later reference.

9. It provides an emergency scanner of text on the page — either copy and paste the text into the Notes app and export as an e-mail, or use the Camera app to take a screen capture (hold the power and Home buttons down simultaneously) and export to e-mail.

10. You can split the touch screen keyboard for thumb-texting, and you can type emoticons (Emoji) and other languages (Settings > General > International > Keyboards).

Setting Up and Organizing Apps into Folders

KEY WEBSITES

- ⌐ http://bit.ly/organize-your-ipad
- ⌐ http://bit.ly/ipad-training
- ⌐ http://bit.ly/organize-apps-on-your-ipad
- ⌐ http://bit.ly/organize-your-iphone-ipad
- ⌐ http://bit.ly/50-best-ipad-apps
- ⌐ http://bit.ly/how-to-arrange-apps-on-ipad

Quotes to Ponder

Organizing ahead of time makes the work more enjoyable.

— Anne Burrell

Organizing is what you do before you do something, so that when you do it, it is not all mixed up.

— A.A. Milne

Definition

Organize: To form into a coherent unity or functioning whole.

— *The Merriam Webster Dictionary*

IT'S CRUCIAL for a person embarking on a long trip to organize the packing, layout, and transport of materials in a suitcase. The same can be said of an entrepreneur using an iPad for the first time. Here are some general tips to remember:

⚙ The iPad comes with a 2-in-1 USB cable charger for computers or the wall outlet. *Don't lose it!* Apple will not replace it for free.

⚙ It's a good idea to charge your iPad when the battery gets down to 10 percent and to totally power down your iPad once a week to refresh.

⚙ You can *sync* your iPad with iTunes so that data is transferred (automatically or manually) from your iTunes library over a USB cable that connects your iPad to your computer. Most people prefer to sync via iCloud so that a backup blueprint of your iPad's contents gets saved regularly. I sync with iTunes when I want to upload music, podcasts, movies, entire photo albums, or read-only PDFs into my iBooks or Doc of the Bay apps.

⚙ Get to know the miscellaneous screen icons and buttons and their different functions: Home, Sleep/Wake, Side Switch (for screen orientation or muting), and Volume.

⚙ Get to know the Settings button intimately so that you can customize the iPad to work and feel the way you want it to by configuring the user-interface for:

- Locking and unlocking the wallpaper
- Setting brightness level
- iCloud backup
- FaceTime and iMessage routing to specific e-mail addresses
- Home sharing ability of your iTunes music library from another computer
- Video access and playback
- Easier navigation using multitasking gestures

- Streaming your iPhoto library so that if you take a photo with your iPad, it will show up on your other Apple devices

- Improved note taking using accessibility features such as automatically setting font type and size

- Automatically downloading purchased apps to all your Apple devices

❀ Protect your iPad three ways:

- Go to Settings > General > Auto Lock to decide when to put your iPad to sleep, which saves the battery

- Go to Settings > General > Passcode Lock to create a password to prevent unwanted access

- Go to Settings > iCloud > Find My iPad and turn this feature on and keep it on so that if you misplace your iPad you can track it (it emits a sound to follow) or lock it from iCloud (to help prevent theft)

❀ You can create and rename your folders multiple times, which is useful since your collection of apps will change over time.

❀ To create a folder, press and hold an app on the Home screen until it shows an x in the top left that wobbles, then drag it onto another app and a folder will be created containing the two apps. Press the Home button to return to the home screen.

❀ The Home button is used to reconfigure folders, access Spotlight Search (press once if you're on the Home screen but twice if you're on any other page), and quit multiple apps that are running in the background and draining power (hit the Home button twice, press the red minus sign, and hit the Home button again twice).

- Create an ongoing backup of your iPad on your computer in iTunes as a safety measure, even if you decide to only use iCloud to back up data, without syncing to a computer. That's okay, because a history and copy of all your purchased apps is stored in iTunes and online in iCloud (Apple's virtual drawer), where you can visit your apps and re-download them to other Apple devices using your Apple ID and password. Make sure that iTunes has a record of *all* of the apps you've purchased in the App Store, whether from your computer or from your iPad, so that you don't lose data or miss out on important, free, sometimes lifesaving updates.

- Go to Settings > iCloud and turn on everything so that your data gets synced.

- To transfer large batches of photos from your library, sync with iTunes.

- To transfer third-party movies, playlists, songs, and individual TV show episodes, sync with your iTunes library on your computer, not just on iCloud, because the original files were not purchased through the iTunes Store and Apple has no record of them.

- To reconfigure folders and upload batches of apps faster, do it in iTunes while your iPad is connected to your computer with the USB cable.

- Use iTunes to access iBooks, and sync read-only copies of PDFs you need as a backup.

- Configure your WiFi access so that you can access your apps. Turn on airplane mode to remove pesky ad pop-ups for many of the free apps found these days.

- Use iCloud to sync your Safari bookmarks, address book (Contacts), and calendar (iCal) information so that you have consistency and backup at the same time.

- ⊛ You can use a Kindle app from Amazon on your iPad to sync your books and PDFs across devices. Some PDF apps sync across all devices using iOS 7.

- ⊛ Remember: If you mistakenly delete an app on your iPad, *it did not get erased* from your virtual drawer online, and you can always re-download it.

- ⊛ You can take screen captures (hold the Power and Home buttons down simultaneously) and/or create Notes for yourself while redesigning the folder layout of your iPad. If you're a new iPad user I suggest that you regularly take screen captures of your folder layout and e-mail them to yourself to keep a diary to look at later. As you get more comfortable and see which apps and app folders are keepers, you'll need fewer visual prompts and reminders.

- ⊛ You *must* be connected to the Internet (and not in airplane mode) to buy an app and/or browse in the iPad App Store.

- ⊛ You *must* have an Apple ID and credit card on file to buy an app. It can be for the iPhone or the iPad — just make sure to click which kind you want.

- ⊛ You should print and review the "iTunes Store Terms and Conditions" and Apple's "Privacy Policy."

- ⊛ You can "buy" free apps at the iPad App Store, which get included in your purchase history.

- ⊛ You can read app reviews and browse content using the iPad App Store.

Penina's Pointers
How to Handle Crashed iOS Apps

1. Close all open apps and start again.

2. Delete the app from the iPad and reload it from your locker/purchase history.

3. Do a hard reset of the iPad (hold the Power and Home buttons down simultaneously).

4. Delete the most recent iCloud backup in the Apple Store, under supervision.

How to Avoid a Scare:
The "iCloud Memory is Full" Notice

1. Keep things running more smoothly by manually turning off the iCloud backup for those apps you don't need to keep track of finished products for, such as certain drawing apps, movie trailers, reference apps, etc. You can do this by going to Settings > iCloud > Storage and Backup > Manage Storage > Pick a Device > Show All Apps and then turning the apps off.

2. Remember: You need a WiFi signal to do this and to have iCloud unobtrusively back up your iPad, which you should do at least once a week when it's plugged in to recharge.

3. You can purchase more iCloud memory from Apple.

4. At the 2013 WWDC Keynote Address on 10 June 2013, it was revealed that Apple is working on iWork for iCloud. It's a new system of sharing and saving

data where you'll be able to access, edit, and store your documents and slideshows online (currently Apple's iWork Suite — Pages, Keynote, and Numbers — is a collection of free apps available for download). However, iWork for iCloud is still in beta as of the end of November 2013. Apple has improved iCloud's real-time organization, download options, and collaboration tools to better compete with other productivity technology such as Google Drive. An online search will yield more information about the pros and cons of Apple's latest offering. I suggest you begin with these links:

- http://bit.ly/apple-iwork-for-icloud
- http://bit.ly/wwdc-2013-keynote
- http://bit.ly/iwork-for-icloud-launches
- http://bit.ly/iwork-for-icloud-reviewed
- http://bit.ly/iwork-icloud-collaboration-tools
- http://bit.ly/iwork-for-icloud-preview
- http://bit.ly/iwork-icloud-collaboration-added

Recommended Cloud Storage Apps for the iPad

Free Apps

- Dropbox
- SugarSync
- Evernote
- Pocket
- Documents by Readdle
- Google Drive
- SkyDrive for Microsoft
- Box.Net
- Memeo Connect for Google Docs
- Good Docs – Google Docs & HTML Editor

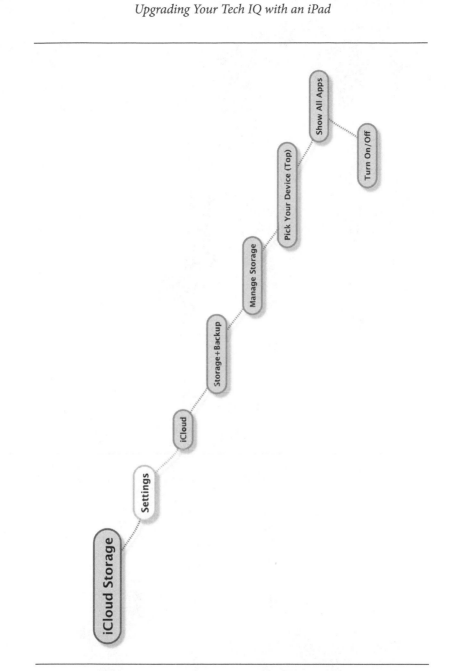

Figure 3-1. Managing iCloud storage for iOS devices. Image created by Penina using the Simple Mind+ app for the iPad.

Paid Apps

⊛ Apple iCloud (5 GB free, but it may pay to buy more)

⊛ GoDocs for Google Drive and Google Docs

For more information on cloud storage options check out the following:

⌐ http://bit.ly/iphone-ipad-cloud-storage-apps

⌐ http://bit.ly/cloud-storage-apps

⌐ http://bit.ly/how-to-free-up-space

⌐ http://bit.ly/cloud-storage-reviewed

⌐ http://bit.ly/personal-cloud-storage-options

Let The Words Flow:
Suggested PDF and Documentation
Apps for Your Workflow

KEY WEBSITES

- http://bit.ly/ipad-pdf-apps
- http://bit.ly/ipad-pdf-annotating-apps
- http://bit.ly/how-to-annotate-ipad-pdf-files
- http://bit.ly/ipad-iphone-pdf-annotation-apps
- http://bit.ly/read-pdfs-on-ipad
- http://bit.ly/ginger-labs-notability
- http://bit.ly/offline-reader-on-itunes
- http://bit.ly/8-best-pdf-apps
- http://bit.ly/100-best-ipad-apps
- http://bit.ly/adobe-reader-on-itunes
- http://bit.ly/free-tools-to-annotate-pdf-docs
- http://bit.ly/best-ipad-apps-2013
- http://bit.ly/265-best-ipad-apps-2013

Quotes to Ponder

Writing and cafes are strongly linked in my brain.

— J. K. Rowling

Colors fade, empires fall, but wise words endure.

— Edward Thorndike

Definition

THE FILE FORMAT *PDF* is used to create documents that can be read on different computer platforms. PDF is the acronym for *Portable Document Format,* created by Adobe in the 1990s and made an open standard, free to the public, in 2008. It's the most popular way to read text and for a PC user to transfer data to a Mac user, including on an iPad.

Let's play a word association game. I say "spreadsheet" and you'll say "___." Probably "Excel" or "database." I say "PDF" and you'll say "___." Perhaps "e-mail?" iPad?" I say "Rowling" and you'll say "___." I hope you said "Harry Potter." The boy who lived. Who made reading fashionable again. Who revolutionized the digital reading experience, just as the iPad is revolutionizing the PDF experience (documentation in today's workplace).

When the iPad made its debut in 2010, many people instinctively knew that the PDF was about to become one of the most crucial linchpins in the app developer industry. In July 2010 Kenneth Kendall, feature editor at the Rutgers University School of Business-Camden, published an article entitled "Continually Emerging Technologies: Will the iPad Change the Way We Live and Work?" (http://bit.ly/will-ipad-change-the-way-we-work).

In the article Kendall writes, "So is the iPad truly a game changer as Apple touts? Does it change the way I conduct my customary business day? The uniqueness of the iPad is having it at the ready in the office and house, anywhere you would like to pick it up and use it." The iPad brought new meaning to the word *portability,* which is one of its key features, benefits, and drawbacks. This portability blurred the lines between personal and professional workflows since the office could now find you and demand your attention and performance by e-mailing you a PDF to peruse.

Kendall also noted, "This version of the iPad is missing a document management system as well as collaboration tools, making it more difficult to produce a collaborative piece than it should be." But in a short time the iPad proved to be the game changer it was predicted to be by allowing third-party apps to fix the collaboration and annotation issues that a portable workflow creates. iPad apps such as Notability, GoodReader, Adobe Reader, and PDFpen, to name a few of the ones I actually use and recommend, have contributed to the paperless culture found in more and more workplaces. Look at the Apple Store model. Kendall summed up his article with these prophetic observations about the iPad: "I do different activities than I typically would on a desktop. For example, I could always have a 'to-do list' on my desktop, but it would remain on my desktop, not where I am when I need to consult it. So, in the end, the iPad has, and will continue to change the way I do my normal routine, my travel, my writing…."

There are entire categories in the App Store today dedicated to catering to the consumer's search for productivity and utility apps. These apps are designed to give the iOS user the ability to use one app for writing notes, another for lists, and still another for PDF use. Here's an example of my own workflow that comes to mind when I lecture about the benefits of iPad use in my seminars.

My go-to app for word processing is Pages, Apple's answer to Microsoft Word. It allows me to integrate media, graphs, and tables within the document and then export the document as either a PDF or Word file. For those wanting quick Dropbox integration and word counts there is PlainText. Many PC users like Textilus, which creates RTF documents for easier formatting with Word. I create most of my lists in Notes, a free, native iOS app with e-mail export and iCloud sync capability. But I also use and love Tree Notepad, my favorite paid app for creating to-do lists as well as outlines and mission statements for projects. It has a built-in calculator and Google search engine portal, which is very convenient for certain meetings and tasks.

As I stated previously, my go-to PDF apps include Notability, GoodReader, Adobe Reader, Doc of the Bay (which uses iTunes syncing and is great for PC users who own an iPad), and PDFpen, which I use when I need a workhorse app for my PDFs. If I want a plain old holding pen for my read-only PDFs, I tend to use the native iBooks, the app that started it all. iBooks has essentially remained the same since it was created — its bookshelf appearance appeals to the busy eye and visual learners in general. Another suggestion is PDFree, which also appeals to the busy eye, visual learners, and people wanting to organize folders of PDFs. People who are auditory learners may like Notability and Paperport Notes for their organizational options and use of the iPad's built-in microphone to record oral notes saved with the individual PDF. The iPad has spawned the iCan era of visual digitalization, facilitating visual learning and execution of tasks, which makes it invaluable to my workflow. The iPad is becoming increasingly essential to me as an educator and speech therapist creating lessons, a presenter showing a stack of slides, and an entrepreneur planning projects, blogposts, and sales pitches, as well as helping me to track and contribute to the social media frenzy.

In fact, the ease of visual presentation using the iPad and the ability to use it for eReader tasks, web browsing, and documentation in either landscape or portrait mode is in keeping with Apple's philosophy of customizing the user interface for each individual. Apple architecture has long been predicated on this principle and has thus lent itself to making the iPad truly versatile. The iPad has indeed revitalized the literacy movement worldwide. Ms. Rowling, our first-grade teachers, and our local librarians would be so proud! The iPad is also helping many people to deliberately or randomly practice acts of sustainability by making it easy to store PDFs, documents, photos, videos, and music in the cloud and to export them via e-mail.

The iPad has thus revitalized the way classrooms and businesses practically apply environmental principles to go green. This phenomenon was written about in *Mashable* in February 2011 by Erica Swallow, who listed three ways iPads help businesses go green: managing energy usage, simplifying environmental auditing, and reducing paper usage (http://bit.ly/ipad-helps-business-go-green). Eco-Libris lists 18 green apps that range from fuel tracking to lighting optimization of your home to stopping junk mail (http://bit.ly/green-apps). And Elizabeth Magill provides a green app roundup in a blogpost that also has links worth checking out (http://bit.ly/apps-to-help-business-go-green).

A 2011 article by Ian Shepherd and Brent Reeves (http://bit.ly/ipad-paperless-classroom) examines the role of the iPad in creating a more mobile, environmentally friendly, and naturalistic learning experience for today's students. The authors wrote that the "iPad with its true mobility has made the paperless classroom practical with its functionality and versatility." I believe the same can be said for the workplace, for businesses large and small, and for the busy entrepreneur whose ability to connect to global markets, and stay connected via e-mails and PDFs, has been greatly enhanced. From reports to meeting minutes, from clipping web pages for later reference to creating to-do lists, iPads are increasingly used to curate content: to generate, revise, store, share, and print text files — namely lists and PDFs — that can be read on almost any digital device. In fact, PDFs are now the most widely accepted format for keeping up with your documents while on the go.

What are the implications for you, the female entrepreneur? There's a story of an Amish farmer who gives his new son-in-law a gift, a toolbox filled with various tools. As the young man lugs the extremely heavy and valuable gift away, his father-in-law calls out, "Don't forget!" The young man responds, "I'll always remember you gave me this wonderful gift." The Amish farmer chidingly replies, "Remember which tool to use when."

iOS apps are tools, like the PDF is a tool, for entrepreneurs to take out, polish, and use as needed. Some apps are native to Apple architecture and will seamlessly work with iCloud syncing and other apps. Some apps are Swiss-army-knife-style apps for the multitasker or startup company on a budget and looking to streamline without compromising quality. Some apps will appeal to a specific learning style or price range. Some apps will be Android/PC friendly, which has it's own appeal. As the saying goes, "there's an app for that," and the next portion of this book will address that further.

Penina's Pointers

Key Workflow Apps for the iPad
(free unless otherwise noted)

To-Do Notes

- Reminders (native)
- Tree Notepad Lite
- MinderBox
- Paper Desk Lite
- Notes by Paperport
- SpringPad
- Sticky Notes FREE
- N+OTES
- Notes (native)
- Paperless Lite
- Cork Board
- Now What
- Mobile Noter
- Upad Lite
- Sticky Notes iPad
- All Stuck Up Lite

PDF Apps

- Notability ($)
- Good Reader ($)
- Neu.Annotate+ PDF ($)
- PDFree
- Paperport Notes
- SmartNote
- SignEasy
- SignNow
- iBooks (native holding pen)
- PDF Pen ($)
- URLtoPDF
- Adobe Reader
- Doc of the Bay
- WEB to PDF
- DocStorm
- PDF Max 2.0
- PDF Splicer

Printer Apps

- Printing for iPad ($)
- ePrint for iPhone ($)
- Air Sharing HD ($)
- DocPrinter ($)
- Print Magic ($)

Word Processing Apps

- Pages
- Documents to Go ($)
- Quickoffice Pro HD ($)
- Daily Notes+ Tasks ($)
- CloudWord-Note Editor
- Textilus Word Processor
- Bdrive for iPad

- iA Writer ($)
- Write 2 ($)
- Plain Text
- Werdsmith
- NOCS
- 7notes HD

Mind Mapping Apps

- MindNode ($)
- Simple Mind+
- Popplet Lite ($ regular)
- MindMeister for iPad
- DropMind Lite by Dooel

- iThoughts HD ($)
- Inspiration Maps Lite
- Headspace Lite
- MindGenius for iPad

Scanner Apps

- Scan
- ScanMyDoc-QR Reader
- JotNot Scanner Pro ($)
- Scanner Pro ($)

- Red Laser iPhone
- DocScan HD
- iRemote Scan

Storage/Portfolio Apps

- DropBox
- Google Docs/Drive
- Pocket
- SpringPad
- Circus Ponies NoteBook ($)

- Sugar Sync
- Amazon Cloud
- Evernote
- Instapaper ($)

Organizational/Documentation iOS Apps Rubric for Entrepreneurs

KEY WEBSITES

- ⌐ http://bit.ly/how-rubrics-help
- ⌐ http://bit.ly/rubric-design-in-ms-word
- ⌐ http://bit.ly/writing-rubrics
- ⌐ http://bit.ly/evaluation-rubrics
- ⌐ http://bit.ly/10-workflow-ios-apps
- ⌐ http://bit.ly/cloud-apps-to-streamline-workflow
- ⌐ http://bit.ly/ipad-apps-for-idea-entrepreneurs
- ⌐ http://bit.ly/ipad-apps-for-entrepreneurs
- ⌐ http://bit.ly/productivity-apps-for-entrepreneurs
- ⌐ http://bit.ly/10-apps-for-entrepreneurs
- ⌐ http://bit.ly/underrated-apps-for-entrepreneurs

Quotes to Ponder

I would be better at my job if I were technical.

— Sheryl Sandberg

The secret of all victory lies in the organization of the non-obvious.

— Marcus Aurelius

Definition

Rubric: A guide listing specific criteria for grading or scoring.

— *The Merriam Webster Dictionary*

A Closer Look:

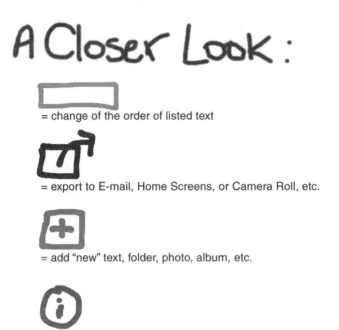

= change of the order of listed text

= export to E-mail, Home Screens, or Camera Roll, etc.

= add "new" text, folder, photo, album, etc.

= find info on this app, including Developer Contact Info, etc.

Figure 3-2. Basic app toolbar. A good app has easy-to-use, easy-to-find features in the toolbar.

RUBRICS are becoming increasingly popular in the worlds of business and education, where outcomes are unfortunately more closely inspected than processes. Rubrics can help you to visualize the components needed to complete tasks or to rule out irrelevant factors. A good rubric can help you figure out if something you were essentially grading, such as a colleague's performance or the efficiency of using a specific technology, is worth it. My app rubric can help you decide which iPad organizational and documentation apps to spend money on. My first rule of thumb is that an app must have a user-friendly toolbar (see Figure 3-2). A good app has easy-to-use, easy-to-find features in the toolbar, allowing you greater flexibility and freedom to do what you do on your projects and to customize a template for variations on a theme as needed. A good app allows you to create data visually and textually, save several copies, make changes easily, and export or share as needed.

Penina's Pointers

Tips for Choosing Which iOS App to Buy and Keep

1. Use an app rubric, maybe even mine (see Figure 3-3), to help determine which features are worth paying for in an app, and then find apps that have those features in their toolbars and settings.

2. Use the built-in features of the App Store app search to help guide your recommendations and browsing history so that you find and purchase apps according to timelines and categories you tend to need and use.

3. Follow a few tech blogs (such as *Macworld* or *iPadInsight*) and do online searches regularly.

4. Get into the habit of browsing the App Store biweekly, looking for free, new, and noteworthy apps that you should have on your radar.

Organizational/Documentation iOS Apps Rubric

TOP 10 FEATURES	Yes	No
I can both type and write (stylus) text.	_____	_____
I can create to-do lists and longer documents.	_____	_____
I can type using different fonts.	_____	_____
I can export via e-mail, Dropbox, etc.	_____	_____
I can draw or sketch with different colors.	_____	_____
I can annotate and export PDFs.	_____	_____
I can intuitively launch and navigate the user interface in timely manner.	_____	_____
I can create folders and tags for filing.	_____	_____
I can clip and attach photos, web content, and URL links.	_____	_____
Online support and guides are available.	_____	_____
TOTAL SCORE (number of Yes answers)	_____ out of 10	

Figure 3-3. Penina's iOS apps rubric. Use Penina's organizational/ documentation iOS apps rubric to help you decide which apps to buy.

How to Streamline E-mail on Your iPad

KEY WEBSITES

- http://bit.ly/ios-adding-email
- http://bit.ly/ios-troubleshooting-mail
- http://bit.ly/how-to-delete-emails-on-ipad
- http://bit.ly/how-to-set-up-email-on-ipad

Quotes to Ponder

If you want something it will elude you. If you don't want something, you will get ten of it in the mail.

— Anna Quindlen

Either write something worth reading, or do something worth writing.

— Benjamin Franklin

Definition

E-mail: A means or system for transmitting messages electronically (as between computers on a network).

— *The Merriam Webster Dictionary*

ELECTRONIC, or digital, mail became ubiquitous around 1993. E-mail is famous for having the @ symbol in the address and containing a subject heading separate from the body of the message. It works similarly to regular mail in that you can see when and from where it was sent, use different stationary or templates, and add attachments. Today you can send letters, photos, music soundbytes, video clips, and even hyperlinks to other people's e-mail addresses. E-mail has greatly enhanced our communication abilities, making our society a truly global one. It has re-energized the struggle to stamp out illiteracy in many countries, improved the workflow of entrepreneurs, and brought together people scattered geographically. But accessing and using e-mail on an iPad is different from accessing and using it on a desktop computer.

Penina's Pointers
Tips for Streamlining E-mail

- Go to Settings > Mail, Contacts, Calendars > Add Accounts to easily add multiple e-mail accounts, streamlining your workflow since your e-mails all come from one source, your Mail app!

- Safeguard your iPad e-mail:
  - Always send a copy of your e-mail to yourself using the Bcc option for safety and records

  - Configure your e-mail accounts using iMap protocols so that your e-mails get stored online as well in the Hotmail, Yahoo, or Gmail Server — extra backup at no extra charge!

  - Have *multiple* e-mail accounts (business, Apple stuff, personal, etc.)

- You will need to decide whether to use the *push* or the *fetch* e-mail features (Settings) to refresh your inbox and how often, depending on your line of work.

- You can delete unwanted e-mail by finger-swiping to the left side or by pressing the Edit button to delete multiple e-mails.

- Go to Settings > Mail > Signature to customize a signature, complete with your contact information, including links to all your social media. This way people will know when you're contacting them from your iPad and will be more understanding of your typos and brevity and won't mind your quick self-promotion at the end of each message, at least not too much.

- You cannot send attachments as you do on a computer. Use the app itself to export files via e-mail. E-mail photos from your camera, PDFs from PDF apps, lists from your Note app or other apps that you may use for quick notes (such as Evernote, Wunderlist, Catch, Tree Notepad, Notability), and docs from the word processing app (such as Pages) that you may end up using.

- Virtual holding pens such as Google Drive, Sugar Sync, and Dropbox are all feasible ways to transfer large files or attachments that can't be traditionally e-mailed. You can do a Google search of these apps to learn more about them.

A Word of Caution About Etiquette and E-mails

I was so excited when I purchased the iPad 2 (I knew the prototype didn't have a camera so I waited). I was determined to improve my typing skills using the native keyboard. I stubbornly refused to buy a case with a built-in keyboard and decided that practicing when sending e-mail was just the ticket. Unfortunately, I learned the hard way that you need to keep in mind that there are rules of etiquette here as well. Rules that I violated, and still do occasionally, despite all that practice my first few months of e-mailing with the iPad. But I learned from my mistakes. So let me share what I learned.

Five Mistakes to Avoid When Typing

1. Typing entirely in capital letters, because the arrow button was accidentally triggered. It's equivalent to shouting. Do so at your own peril, especially when composing business-related e-mails. People read them and think you're either angry with them or insulting their intelligence when you stress words, or worse, the entire message.

2. Hitting the Send button prematurely, or worse, sending your e-mail to the wrong person and wondering at a lack of response. Watch your fingers!

3. Ignoring the native spell check, that tendency of the iPad to auto-correct for you, sometimes hilariously, sometimes to your detriment. On the flip side, you can have fun with that by putting a disclaimer at the end of your e-mail's signature. I have one for e-mail sent with my iPhone (see Figure 3-4).

4. Composing a title header for your e-mail's subject that's longer than the box you were given to type it in. No one wants to read the entire header in that box. Your e-mail will get lost in the shuffle of other e-mails as the reader ignores your irrelevant, verbose wording.

5. Signing off the same way you do on your phone or desktop when checking e-mail. Have a signature that includes "sent from my iPad" so that you observe this most crucial and as-of-yet unspoken rule of etiquette. People need to know that the e-mail originated from your iPad in case it was short, terse, misspelled, the attachment didn't get forwarded properly, or you (gasp) rushed to type a response, in capital letters, in the subject box, in auto-correct mode, letting your iPad merrily and quietly sabotage your best efforts to be polite and professional.

●●●●○ Verizon 📶   11:40 AM   @ ✳ 87% ▬▬)

Cancel   **New Message**   Send

Penina Rybak
Sent from my iPhone en route

👍Typos due to Siri not self
regulated--Socially Speaking™
Protocol on Standby. 3️⃣ 2️⃣ 1️⃣ 👍

Penina Rybak MA/CCC-SLP
CEO Socially Speaking LLC
Director: The NICE Initiative
Email: penina@niceinitiative.com,
penina.sociallyspeaking@gmail.com
Website: sociallyspeakingllc.com,
niceinitiative.com
Twitter: @PopGoesPenina
Work # (646) 820-5547

Figure 3-4. Penina's iOS signature. This humorous signature was created by Penina using Apple's Emoji keyboard setting for iOS devices.

Internet and iPad Use — Surf Smart

KEY WEBSITES

- http://bit.ly/safari-browse-the-web
- http://bit.ly/how-to-use-safari
- http://bit.ly/how-to-browse-internet-on-ipad
- http://bit.ly/chrome-for-ipad-better-than-safari
- http://bit.ly/chrome-browser-app
- http://bit.ly/dolphin-browser-for-ipad
- http://bit.ly/best-web-browsers-for-ipad

Quotes to Ponder

Our free enterprise system of disseminating information is collectively referred to as The Media. But there is no collective.

— Jessica Savitch

Whoever controls the media, controls the mind.

— Jim Morrison

Definition

Internet: An electronic communications network that connects computer networks and organizational computer facilities around the world.

— *The Merriam Webster Dictionary*

THE INTERNET'S PROGENITOR, ARPANET, began in the early 1960s as a closed network between a few universities conducting research. It would develop and expand throughout the 1960s and 1970s until 1981, when the concept of a world-wide network of interconnected networks, called the Internet, was introduced. The advent of the personal computer in the late 1970s and 1980s would change the Internet from a research tool to a communication tool. But it was the introduction in 1991 of the World Wide Web, a system of hypertext documents accessed via the Internet and viewed by a web browser, that would lead to the Internet becoming known as the "information superhighway."

A few pioneers such as Mark Andreessen, creator of the first popular web browser, Netscape Navigator, in 1994 (which was transformed into Mozilla Firefox in 2002), Bill Gates, who gave the okay to release the browser Microsoft Internet Explorer in 1995, and Steve Jobs, who unveiled the Apple Safari Browser in 2003, have been instrumental in changing the face of the Internet. Surfing the net was initially a static, cumbersome process. Computer users had to have dial-up service to connect to the net, usually at very slow modem speeds, through their telephone lines.

I remember hearing jarring noises (which was normal), when trying to connect to the Internet to check my America Online e-mail and browse the web, before Web 2.0 was released in 1999. Before that the web didn't have the ability to host the social media, multimedia, tags, blogs, bookmarks, and holding pen sites supported today through JavaScript and Flash. Examples of Web 2.0 are Yahoo's Flickr or Pinterest, both of which store and share digital photos. Web 2.0 has given digital photo and library services, cloud computing services, IT outsourcing services, special education, and especially entrepreneurship second chances for global distribution.

The Internet behaves like a sentient entity, just as science fiction movies and books predicted! That was even before the release of the iPhone in 2007, which changed the game yet again in terms of Internet use. The release of the Google Chrome browser in 2008 and the iPad in 2010 further pushed the envelope. Web and app developers are becoming celebrities, courted as rigorously as politicians and diplomats.

The Safari browser, native to Apple architecture, is many iPad users' browser of choice because of how seamlessly it's integrated into iPad's overall user interface. I prefer it when surfing the net because Safari lets me:

⚙ Turn on private browsing (bottom left of open Safari window) and Clear History (Settings > Safari).

⚙ Use the Reader option to read it later (Add to Reading List).

⚙ Configure my bookmarks, add sites to bookmarks, or add sites to my home screen.

⚙ E-mail the link of the website that interests me so I can share it with others.

As mentioned in Chapter 2, I happen to like using the Firefox browser when searching for video and music clips for my projects. I don't use it on any of my mobile devices, but only on my desktop computer, which happens to be an iMac. I also sometimes use the Google Chrome browser, but only to:

⚙ Do voice searches by tapping a small microphone icon.

⚙ Use incognito mode (a spy-man icon will appear in the top left corner of the window) which is like private browsing for Safari.

I stopped using the Internet Explorer browser years ago, and my PC desktop is happily virus-free. It's also currently in storage.

When asked which Internet-based apps for the iPad I recommend for entrepreneurs, I promptly rattle off this list, my top ten:

1. Zite
2. Evernote
3. Pocket
4. SoundHound
5. Haiku Deck
6. Cooliris (also for desktops)
7. Pinterest
8. Google+
9. TED
10. Kindle

Penina's Pointers

Tips for Enhancing Your Web-Surfing Experience

1. There are apps that help you with storage, such as Pocket and Evernote, which are both free, and Instapaper and Circus Ponies, which cost money but may be worth it if you're part of a Mac network with at least one Mac desktop. They all act as holding pens for content that you've read online.

2. There are websites and services that come with apps to help you access your stored data, which you need to back up regularly online in case your iPad crashes. I'm referring to Cloud services (free unless noted) such as:

   - Google Drive
   - Amazon Cloud Drive
   - JustCloud.com ($)
   - Microsoft SkyDrive ($)
   - DropBox
   - SugarSync
   - Zip Cloud ($)
   - Backup Genie ($)

3. Your Safari browser has a print option for web pages you want to share.

4. Bookmarks in Safari do not come preloaded, and the bookmarking process is a bit different for your iPad vs. your desktop computer.

Tips for Creating Bookmarks in Safari with Your iPad

1. Go to Settings > Safari > Always Enable Bookmarks Bar.

2. Tap the + button in the Safari Navigation Bar > Add Bookmark.

3. In the Add Bookmark window you can add a website to your list of bookmarks or store it inside the bookmarks bar for later viewing. These sites will then appear each time you open your Safari browser under the Safari Navigation Menu.

4. Remember to turn iCloud and the bookmarks tab on so that you sync all your bookmarks between all your Apple devices!

A Picture Paints a Thousand Words: How Entrepreneurs Should Use Photos

KEY WEBSITES

- http://pinterest.com
- https://twitter.com
- http://images.google.com
- http://picasa.google.com
- http://www.photobucket.com
- http://www.flickr.com
- http://www.snapfish.com
- http://bit.ly/ipad-photo-sharing-apps
- https://www.dropbox.com
- http://bit.ly/snapseed-on-itunes
- http://bit.ly/how-to-download-photos-to-ipad
- http://bit.ly/add-delete-photos-from-computer-to-ipad
- http://www.briansolis.com
- http://bit.ly/andrea-vascellari-blog
- http://bit.ly/jay-deragon-blog
- http://www.personalbrandingblog.com

Quotes to Ponder

A very subtle difference can make the picture or not.
— Annie Leibovitz

Of all our inventions for mass communication, pictures still speak the most universally understood language.
— Walt Disney

Definition

Photo: A picture or likeness. A shortened version of the term photograph.

— The Merriam Webster Dictionary

Louis Daguerre and George Eastman have been the proclaimed fathers of photography since the 1800s. But it really wasn't until the 1990s, when the digital camera was born, that most people could actually sit in the driver's seat for the whole trip, from taking the picture to having the final product. With a digital camera people could tap into their artistic side and technological side simultaneously. They could photograph in color or black and white and then go home to back up cherished memories to their hard drives. People could edit their photos themselves and save them to virtual albums at half the cost. The photo became an official soldier in the Tech Revolution, thanks to the work of people at the Kodak company, who introduced the concept of developing photos on a CD, not just on film.

I remember using the Apple Quick Take 100 Camera, which hit stores in 1994, and the Sony Cyber Shot Digital Still Camera, which made its debut in 1996, when I participated in the New York State TRAID Project spearheaded by the Westchester Institute of Human Development. Our goal was to train special educators, occupational therapists, speech therapists like myself, and school-based administrators to implement assistive technology, namely Apple tech, into special education classrooms and curriculums. As an Apple techie and visual learner, I began my personal odyssey to become part of the Tech Revolution.

When the iPhone was launched in 2007, the game and the players changed again. Photography was revolutionized once more. The subsequent introduction of the consumer to the iTunes App Store five years ago again changed the way photography is integrated into our daily lives. Social media are constantly evolving, but our appetite for a visual representation of our own realities is keeping pace.

Which leads us to the question: Is a snapshot of you or your work posted online indicative of your reality or of the reality you're trying to create? Here's another question to ponder: Does your digital reputation online provide an accurate snapshot of your behavior in real time? Coming to grips with the answers to these questions is why balancing humanity and technology is so crucial for you, and why digital crisis intervention is becoming increasingly important. And it's why I regular follow the writings of thought leaders like Brian Solis, Jay Deragon, Andrea Vascellari, Dan Schawbel, Diane Bertolin, Charlene Li, and Beth Kanter on the impact of social technology on entrepreneurship and marketing trends.

A Picture Paints a Thousand Words … in Pixels

SHORTLY AFTER the leg of the Tech Revolution involving photos was underway, a shift in thinking happened. The line between personal/private and public/political photography blurred yet again. The catalyst was 9/11. War correspondents and photographers have been around for decades — just look at *Life* magazine. Yet on September 11, 2001, average people were put front and center of the action. Anyone who took a photo and posted it online became an official 9/11 storyteller. And, in addition to the obvious social, psychological, economic, historical, and political repercussions to 9/11 that we all know about, there was the incubation of new soldiers in the Tech Revolution in a petri dish. Called the millennial generation, it's becoming the largest marketing demographic and group of entrepreneurs to date.

This is important to know because millennials in particular are causing us to change the way we approach our work/life balance, approach entrepreneurship, engage in social media, do business, advertise in cyber time and real time, and create with and consume visual media (art, film, books, blogs, mobile technology). The push for the digitalization of visual content marketing to drive commerce can be traced to tech savvy and a love for "selfies" (self-portraits). Visual content marketing is becoming increasingly popular and is now regularly analyzed around the water cooler at work, in the blogosphere, and at business seminars. Two new buzzwords — *visuals* and *storytelling* — are subsequently on the lips of many fellow entrepreneurs.

Marshall McLuhan said, "Advertising is the greatest art form of the twentieth century." That includes visual trends such as "food porn" on Pinterest and "selfies" on Instagram, the two fastest growing social media channels of 2013. They house digital photos, videos, infographics, and links and tips regarding mobile apps that contain icons, comics, and even mind maps. Which brings me to these ideas I took away from the Business Development Institute's Visual Social Communications Leadership Forum in New York on 12 December 2013. The forum happened because Founder/CEO Steve Etzler and Director of Events Maria Feola-Magro worked together seamlessly to provide a condensed, live opportunity for networking, collaboration, thought leadership, and learning best practices for today's fast-paced, tech-savvy, busy professionals. Three common themes in social media emerged with these questions being raised again and again:

1. How can you leverage visuals more meaningfully to drive social media traffic and engagement?

2. When should you feed the social media beast: in cyber time after social listening (or not, as Lululemon Athletica did by ignoring complaints about one of its women's yoga pants being see-through causing a huge outcry) or in real time, when a news event occurs or something trending goes viral? (Think what Oreo brilliantly did at the 2013 Super Bowl during the blackout, tweeting an ad in the third quarter proclaiming that "You can still dunk in the dark.")

3. Why is repurposing content (self- or user-generated) using visuals across miscellaneous social channels psychologically effective for branding and eliciting calls to action?

A picture really does tell a story. When done right, seeding visuals into your social media pipeline or feed can drive (short-term) but also sustain (long-term) consumer loyalty, provide opportunities for more authentic, organic engagement with followers, help facilitate more consistent brand recognition and advocacy, help you repurpose previously posted textual content for greater retention and emotional impact, generate a call to action that simultaneously entertains and inspires, lengthen your service's or product's virtual shelf life, and entice people from all demographics to cross-pollinate their "shares" and "likes." This last point is the elephant in the room, the conundrum that so many entrepreneurs and advertising agencies face today when trying to leverage social media to generate revenue for services and products and turn leads (bystanders) into bona fide customers (evangelists). In practical terms, visual content marketing is feasible as long as you understand:

- The need for active, ongoing content curation using a physical (iPhoto for Mac, external hard drive) as well as a cloud-based (Pocket or Evernote apps, Pinterest boards, Dropbox, SugarSync) holding pen for your pictures.

- The elements of humor and storytelling, which provide the tracks underneath the social media train transporting your visuals.

- The value in posting visual content more than once on your feed to trigger and sustain an emotional reaction, and in posting these visuals thematically, using elements of doing good, social entrepreneurship, and branding.

- The importance of sustaining engagement in one venue before jumping on another that's trending.

- The power of customizing your visual hook to reach people in niche markets based on knowing what makes them tick, where they hang out, and what interests them. Which brings me back to the demographic that's puzzling so many thought leaders, CEOs, and employers — the millennials.

Are You Picture Ready?

GENERATION Y, also known as the millennial generation, is the generation born between 1980 and 2000. They were either directly affected by the events of 9/11 or indirectly affected by the vibes around them from those who were. The events of 9/11, which I lived through as an adult, have affected the way we live, from the deployment of our loved ones overseas to the way we pack our carry-on luggage and board a plane.

Another significant effect of 9/11 is that it produced the largest think tank and focus group for technology trends in the world. One that deployed average people, even children, to contribute to the informal research. To have an impact through photography on world opinion and social consciousness. The modern-day artist and war correspondent was born.

As stated previously, I believe in patterns, that nothing is random. It's no coincidence that the millennial generation made Instagram, launched in October 2010, the most popular photo-sharing app for the iPhone today. I would love to get insight from the Freakonomics Duo on this! Instagram is an iPhone app that allows you to alter the appearance of your photo and share it in a photo stream that can be re-shared and followed by others. It's described in the App Store as "a simple way to make and share gorgeous photos on your iPhone. Transform everyday moments into works of art you'll want to share with friends and family." It's free, fun, and easy to use. What's not to like?

In March 2013 a survey was published in a Brafton editorial piece for entrepreneurs and others trying to improve their marketing skills (http://bit.ly/millennials-use-instagram). The article stated that the millennial generation comprises the largest portion of users of Instagram. The author quoted statistics and went on to write, "This data should come as no surprise to the savvy marketer. Immature and youthful social networks often attract younger markets first, as these people are most likely to try new social hubs and then tell their parents or other connections about the service." New patterns and niche markets are emerging based upon shifts in demographics and technology trends. The Hubspot blog is great to monitor in general, but especially in regard to millennials. A long-term-thinking, analytical entrepreneur who's interested in inbound content marketing and niche marketing should observe millennials and also take a look at Dan Schawbel's book, *Promote Yourself,* and these articles:

- ✓ http://bit.ly/how-to-build-successful-career
- ✓ http://bit.ly/gen-y-in-mood-to-buy-houses
- ✓ http://bit.ly/how-millennials-think
- ✓ http://bit.ly/adjust-marketing-tactics-for-millennials
- ✓ http://bit.ly/the-me-generation
- ✓ http://bit.ly/millennials-ending-9-to-5
- ✓ http://bit.ly/new-face-of-diversity
- ✓ http://bit.ly/is-gen-y-lazy
- ✓ http://bit.ly/millennials-working-with-older-colleagues

Members of the millennial generation, more than previous ones (and no, I'm not a millennial), are truly catalysts for promoting change. The Entrepreneurial Revolution has intersected with the Tech Revolution largely because of them and their creative, collaborative leanings. The next wave of entrepreneurial ventures will focus on social entrepreneurship mainly because of them and their desire to give back to the community. I've trained and worked with wonderful millennials for years. I've engaged in both career mentorship and technology-based reverse mentorship in educational, healthcare, and corporate arenas and I've seen that this generation is often maligned and misunderstood. Remember Joel Stein's controversial article in *Time* magazine?

In May 2013 millennials were in the limelight, and entrepreneurs and marketers around the country sat up and took note. *Time* magazine ran a pivotal, controversial article and cover about the millennial generation entitled, "The Me Me Me Generation." Author Joel Stein wrote that "millennials are just adapting quickly to a world undergoing rapid technological change." He reported that members of this generation, more than previous ones, are the most comfortable in front of a camera and more likely to visually record and post online the various mundane details of their lives. He got much attention, good and bad, for writing that this generation's overall incidence of narcissistic personality disorder is nearly three times higher than their grandparents' generation. The article appeared in print and online for paid subscribers of the magazine.

The article has since gone viral, as have many comments and rebuttals. It's understandable that many baby boomers have found fault with the millennial generation. I found the article somewhat unidimensional and short-sighted and want to address the perks, wisdom, strengths, and headaches a millennial employee, entrepreneur, or colleague brings to the table.

I've mentored many professional women millennials. I've given seminars and spoken at length with people in this group. One of my brothers is a millennial, and I've learned much from his outlook and performance. My perception of millennials continues to morph, but as an entrepreneur I recommend two specific plans of action for you regarding millennials:

- As an entrepreneur in a tech-driven, ever-changing global market, you need to emulate some millennial behaviors as best practices.

- You need to find ways to deploy your hook (to effect change and implement your own mission statement) by seeking to actively target, court, and collaborate with this demographic, which should not be marginalized as a limited sampling. It has already become a powerful niche market.

Here are some inflammatory statements written by Stein in his *Time* magazine article that made me pause to consider. I partially disagree with them based on the millennials I know. Here are the statements I think entrepreneurs need to analyze, and determine the validity of, for their own marketing strategies, whatever service or product they're providing:

- ❀ "Millennials are interacting all day but almost entirely through a screen."

- ❀ "They might look calm, but they're deeply anxious about missing out on something better."

- ❀ "Not only do millennials lack the kind of empathy that allows them to feel concerned for others, but they also have trouble even intellectually understanding others' points of view."

- ❀ "What they do understand is how to turn themselves into brands."

- ❀ "Millennials perceived entitlement isn't a result of overprotection, but an adaptation to a world of abundance."

- ❀ "Companies are starting to adjust, not just to millennials' habits, but also to their atmospheric expectations."

- ❀ "They are tinkerers more than dreamers, life hackers."

- ❀ "A generation's greatness isn't determined by data; it's determined by how they react to the challenges that befall them. And, just as important, by how we react to them."

Penina's Pointers

The Importance of Protecting Your Digital Reputation

Why am I sharing all this information on Stein's article with you? Because even though I don't agree with all the points raised in the article, I did learn an important lesson. An entrepreneur needs to know about the politics of the playground, so to speak, about the niche markets, the theory of mind (empathy and perspective), and the connection between the two. People passionate about their photos are certainly ones you'll want to target using social media tools such as Instagram and Pinterest. Demographics play a huge role in marketing. Know your audience — their favorite hangouts, in real time and online, and their foibles. Know yours as well. Your knowledge of your audience can impact effective communication and make or break a deal.

It's important to understand the sandbox you're playing in and who the key players are who are sharing your space. Who will hopefully notice you and share their shovels and cups with you. For further information, I recommend that you read *Ready, Fire, Aim* by Michael Masterson. I especially like the twenty lessons listed in Chapter 15, "Aiming the Marketing." (#1: "Always remember customers don't care about your company. They care about themselves.") The book is basic common sense, providing an easy-to-understand, hierarchal framework that I found illuminating and succinct.

A little narcissism is actually good. Introspection about your personal learning style and tech IQ, which can be synthesized and harnessed as a combustible combination, will help you in the long run. A bit of narcissism can fuel your creativity and social media success. Not harnessing that power, by not doing your homework about yourself or about the technology you need to succeed, can negatively impact your reputation, in real time or online. Learning about yourself, about your strengths and weaknesses, will help you tap into your potential. A bit of narcissism combined with your tech savvy can profoundly impact your future as an entrepreneur. Part of your sterling reputation depends on:

- What you can do with technology to further marketing and selling your service or product

- What your digital footprint, your social media presence, reveals about you, on and off the playground

One of the specialists at the Apple Store I frequent at the Garden State Plaza Mall in Paramus, New Jersey, said, "A mistake recorded online gets archived for all time." It made me realize that I would have to ponder each word, picture, and link I post. That I needed to make my personal posts to friends and family undetectable. That I need to be vigilant about not being commented about or tagged in someone else's posts, especially controversial ones! I was reminded again of the importance of being vigilant a few months ago, when a friend accidentally mentioned me in a potentially insulting post. She wrote that I also once said the same thing about so and so. While it may have been true, I had to call her and explain that it was said in jest, and in private! I made her take my name off her comment. It prompted me to really think about the dos and don'ts of creating social media content, which I scribbled on a napkin and then noted in my Evernote. Let me share my list.

Ten Mistakes to Avoid When Creating a
Digital Footprint

1. Posting revealing or impolite photos of or comments about yourself in compromising positions (Here's your litmus test: Would you want your grandparents and parents to see this?)

2. Posting inappropriate or rude photos, links, or content of others engaged in questionable behavior (see litmus test above)

3. Posting vocabulary and/or content that's culturally insensitive or rude (Would you want your young child, or you as a child, reading the post?)

4. Using phraseology and terminology, including slang, that's offensive and/or untrue

5. Plagiarizing phraseology, terminology, or content

6. Coming across as arrogant in your choice of photo or the wording in your post

7. Coming across as fluffy by not posting enough thought-provoking photos or content about your mission

8. Coming across as sloppy or distracted by posting a photo that's upside down or blurry or content that's misspelled or poorly written

9. Not posting frequently, so that you're inefficient in nourishing the seeds that you've planted

10. Not breaking up your posts into daily themes, so that your followers lack a cohesive framework to follow and re-post for you.

Ten Visual Storytelling Tips for Social Media Marketing

1. Photos should tell a tale, with or without text depending on your target audience and platform. If using text, use an iPad app like Over to add text to your photos.

2. Photo size, category, or type should be tailored to the specific channel the photo is displayed on. Mix it up: use static photos with text on Facebook, glossier and larger photos without text on Pinterest, enhanced selfies on Instagram, short video clips on YouTube and Vimeo, even shorter ones on Vine, repurposed photos and infographics on Google+, Twitter, and Wordpress and Tumblr blogs, and links to blogs on all venues, including LinkedIn and e-mail newsletters.

3. Photos should be displayed as a result of social listening first, then devising a content strategy.

4. Photos should amplify the emotional message you're trying to convey and the brand you're trying to promote.

5. Photos should include a call to action in a message format that's simple and that sticks (see Chapter 4 on storytelling for more information).

6. Photos should be curated and tagged by you and your followers to provide a more authentic user interface.

7. Photos should be easily seen across all mobile technology platforms and open in different apps without a negative change in formatting.

8. Photos should be posted in thematic units to provide context and flow to your posts.

9. Photos should be posted with hashtags for easier sharing and nurturing of the thread in your posts.

10. Photos should be yours, licensed, or permitted under the current laws of fair use.

Key Photo-Sharing Apps for the iPad
(free unless otherwise noted)

- Pinterest
- Pic Jointer
- Booth Free
- My Sketch
- Red Stamp for iPhone
- PictNote Free for iPhone
- Photogram for iPhone
- Photogene ($)

- Pic Collage
- Collage
- Pic Stitch
- Pixlr-o-matic
- WhiteBoard
- Color Effects
- Jot! Free
- Comic Life ($)

Key Camera Apps for the iPad
(free unless otherwise noted)

- Camera (native)
- Instagram for iPhone
- Perfect Photo for iPhone
- Adobe Photoshop Express
- Pixlr-o-matic
- Photo Card Lite
- Simply B&W
- Photo Toon LT for iPhone
- Photo Booth (native)
- Secure My Privacy
- TourWrist
- Photogene ($)

- Photos (native)
- CamWow for iPhone
- Cooliris
- Pic Collage
- My Sketch
- Photo Editor
- PM Mosaic for iPhone
- Photosynth for iPhone
- Private Photo Vault
- Vintage Camera
- iPhoto ($)
- PhotoSync ($)

Notes from the Business Development Institute's 2013 Visual Social Communications Leadership Forum

Kristie Wells Visual Communications Formula:

Engagement Ratio = Number of posts divided by interactions (comments + likes + shares)

Content Strategy Objectives

1. Build awareness (20%) by posting across social platforms

2. Educate members (78%) by providing tips on the topic at hand and infographics

3. Drive conversion (2%) by driving sentiment posting humorous and emotive visuals: e-cards, current events pics, pop culture references.

Amanda Pehrson's Pinterest Pointers

1. Content curation is key. It fuels branding in a less in-your-face way regarding calls to action.

2. Finding influencers and advocates helps you partner, repurpose, grow, and collaborate with others on your story.

3. Customized sweepstakes drive traffic and engagement via click-throughs.

4. Custom advertorials use these elements of great stories: culture, style, simplicity, authenticity, conversation, connectivity.

5. Document the process: Be a journalist about your own endeavors, your successes and failures, your story.

Aaron Clossey's Road Map to Better Visual Content Marketing

Pinterest Road Map

1. Cover your bases: Provide visually compelling content that's optimized for pinners (plug-ins, site layout, Pin It buttons, etc.).

2. Stand put: Resize your visuals and provide textual overlays and calls to action where needed.

3. Mix it up: Pin your visuals as a mixture of still photos and video clips. Also share the pins of others to drive interest and engagement.

4. Embrace your influencers: Ask them to curate content. Identify relevant verticals you want to tap into, and establish long-term brand evangelism.

5. Fuel inspiration: Find your sweet spot and hold on! Rally the community around a passion point through Pinterest-exclusive contests.

Instagram Road Map

1. Real-time posting is key: Capitalize on what's trending.

2. Visual integration is both an art and science: Provide authentic visuals that tug at heart strings and humanize the message with labels, attribution, and text overlays of scenes, *not* selfies.

3. Empower influencers, advocates, and colleagues to curate content for you via e-mail forms with submission guidelines and call-to-action hashtags.

4. Recognize and reward your advocates and targeted audiences in ways that are valuable in targeting them, and tie your brand directly to these consumer experiences.

Best Practices in Visual Content Marketing

Check out my blog post on visual content marketing (http://bit.ly/social-media-train), where I cite best practices as well as specific books and articles for you to read for more information.

Thanks to the following people, whose thought leadership helped me sequence and more methodically compile this list: Aaron Clossey, Jon Fox, Jessica Lauria, Amanda Pehrson, Michael Pranikoff, Stephanie Scott, and Kristie Wells, all experts in their fields and speakers at the BDI Visual Social Communications Leadership Forum on 12 December 2013, and a special thanks to Maria Feola-Magro for finding them.

Websites to Help You Increase Your Tech IQ with an iPad

KEY WEBSITES

- http://bit.ly/50-ipad-tips
- http://bit.ly/ipad-tips-and-tricks
- http://bit.ly/14-ipad-tips
- http://www.ipadtips.org/
- http://bit.ly/imore-tips-and-how-tos
- http://bit.ly/complete-list-of-ipad-tips-tutorials
- http://bit.ly/100plus-ipad-tips
- http://bit.ly/ipad-news-reviews
- http://bit.ly/mashable-software-and-apps
- http://bit.ly/lifehacker-app-directory
- http://bit.ly/make-googleplus-hangouts-your-meeting-room
- http://bit.ly/browse-macworld
- http://bit.ly/ted-ideas-worth-spreading
- https://www.dropbox.com/
- https://www.sugarsync.com/
- http://bit.ly/amazon-cloud-drive
- http://www.padgadget.com/
- http://www.apple.com/ipad/
- http://www.engadget.com/
- http://bit.ly/skype-for-ipad
- http://bit.ly/ilounge-apple-support
- http://bit.ly/ipad-camera-connection-kit-connects-other-things
- http://bit.ly/cnet-tablets-how-to

- http://www.theipadguide.com/
- http://bit.ly/cult-of-mac-app-finder
- http://bit.ly/osxdaily-on-ipad
- http://ipadacademy.com/
- https://www.stumbleupon.com
- http://www.makeuseof.com/
- http://bit.ly/everbuying-ipad-accessories
- http://www.freecycle.org/
- http://bit.ly/goodnight-ipad-childrens-book
- http://bit.ly/getting-started-with-evernote
- http://bit.ly/ginger-labs-notability
- http://bit.ly/apple-ipad-support
- http://bit.ly/apple-ipad-user-guide
- http://bit.ly/awesome-ipad-tips
- http://bit.ly/engadget-for-ipad
- http://www.cnet.com/
- http://bit.ly/best-ipad-tips
- http://bit.ly/free-ipad-apps
- http://bit.ly/pocket-lint-ipad-news
- http://bit.ly/ipad-free-software
- http://bit.ly/kindle-for-ipad-help
- http://bit.ly/pcmag-100-best-ipad-apps
- http://bit.ly/voice-recording-apps
- http://ipadinsight.com

Quotes to Ponder

I'm totally obsessed with technology.

— Jodi Picoult

Never ask what sort of computer a guy drives. If he's a Mac user, he'll tell you. If not, why embarrass him?

— Tom Clancy

Definition

Website: A group of World Wide Web pages usually containing hyperlinks to each other and made available online by an individual, company, educational institution, government, or organization.

— *The Merriam Webster Dictionary*

WEBSITES represent the stops along the Information Superhighway. They are the chief means of digital information sharing for many of us today. A good website appeals to both sides of your brain. It has graphics, links, thought-provoking content, and an easy-to-navigate legend or key, like the one on a map, to help you view all there is to see on that site. Websites can be bookmarked and saved for later reference. Links to a website can be e-mailed, shared via social media, and found in search engine listings in browsers such as Google, Yahoo, Bing, and Dolphin for iPad. A website, and its creator, is only as visible as the content used to create it. More and more people are becoming public figures, in both real time and online by creating websites for social media, education, business, daily living, and entertainment purposes. Websites provide a multisensory and engaging learning experience for people accessing a variety of information on the Internet. They've had a large impact on the globalization of our economy, the way school curriculums are deployed, and the way we live our lives today. Usage patterns of websites vary with geographical location, demographics, and purpose of access. But educational institutions, world markets, libraries, and even entrepreneurs need to change the way research, marketing, and communication are done.

Penina's Pointers

Implications for Entrepreneurs: Make the Web Work for You!

1. It's time to learn how to use a search engine like Google more effectively. Improve your time management and research skills. This infographic may help: http://bit.ly/use-google-search-effectively.

2. It's time to create a portfolio (a digital folder or holding pen), using apps such as Zite, Pocket, and/or Evernote, to save links from iPad-related websites to increase your tech IQ.

    - http://www.zite.com
    - http://getpocket.com
    - http://bit.ly/how-to-use-evernote

3. It's time to peruse and save links to websites that are designed for, have content about, or promote a product or service similar to yours. Study your competition, legally (http://bit.ly/12-ways-to-spy-on-competitors).

4. It's time to create a digital footprint, or improve the one you have, using social media appropriately and in appropriate venues. Get noticed! Start by creating a website. I use Sandvox for mine, but there are other

programs to choose from. There are also various social media sites to choose from, and here are links to get you started:

- http://www.linkedin.com
- http://bit.ly/build-your-resume-on-linkedin
- http://bit.ly/guide-to-social-media-marketing
- http://bit.ly/facebook-quick-guide
- http://bit.ly/facebook-marketing-guide
- http://bit.ly/create-a-googleplus-business-page
- http://bit.ly/generate-leads-with-googleplus
- http://bit.ly/use-googleplus-for-business
- http://bit.ly/googleplus-guide-for-everyone
- http://bit.ly/guide-to-pinterest
- http://bit.ly/promote-your-website-with-pinterest
- http://bit.ly/marketing-with-pinterest
- http://bit.ly/ultimate-guide-to-pinterest
- http://bit.ly/pinterest-primer
- http://bit.ly/set-up-a-youtube-channel
- http://www.slideshare.net

Books to Help You Increase Your Tech IQ with an iPad

KEY WEBSITES

- http://www.amazon.com
- http://www.publiclibraries.com
- http://www.gutenberg.org
- http://freecomputerbooks.com
- http://www.scribd.com
- http://onlinebooks.library.upenn.edu
- http://www.questia.com
- http://openlibrary.org
- http://www.readprint.com

Quotes to Ponder

If you read a lot of books, you are considered well-read. But if you watch a lot of TV, you're not considered well-viewed.

— Lily Tomlin

Some books leave us free, and some books make us free.

— Ralph Waldo Emerson

Definition

Book: A set of written, printed, or blank sheets bound together in a volume. Something that yields knowledge or understanding.

— *The Merriam Webster Dictionary*

'M A READER. I asked for a library card at age three. I still think libraries are magical places. I recommend them to others, even in this day and age. I frequently haunt my local library and bookstore. Perusing the Amazon home page is on my daily to-do list. My childhood was spent reading physical books. Later on I read a bit differently, but I was still reading. Real library books and e-books on my Kindle, and then my Kindle app for my iOS devices, and then subscribing to and reading RSS feeds, all of which became a prominent staple in my adult workflow. But I haven't left the actual paper book behind. In fact, as a special education teacher, turned speech therapist, turned educational technology consultant, turned entrepreneur, I have found that reading a physical book, turning its pages, and holding it in my hands facilitates muscle memory. This in turn fosters episodic memory, allowing me to link the vocabulary I read and learn with the event and experience of using that book to do so. The result is better retention of the material I read. I try to get the same effect from my e-book experience by using bookmark and highlighter features to help me internalize subject matter and recall it later on.

The Case for Reading

READING is more than a pastime or parental directive from childhood. It's a crucial activity that students hone with practice over time. For an entrepreneur, who is essentially a student of life, reading is essential, because it keeps you curious. It keeps you in the learning zone so that you don't get complacent. So that you keep testing your limits, pushing the envelope professionally and personally to continuously grow socially and intellectually.

A reader stays current and constantly expands his or her theory of mind. A reader develops an extensive working lexicon, an increased attention span, and more linear thought processes. These are important traits for you to have as an entrepreneur. If you don't read books on a variety of subjects regularly, but especially in the areas relevant to your product or service, you run the risk of becoming stagnant in your outlook, in the execution and performance of your tasks, and in your overall sentience as a human being. The act of reading has both a calming and stimulating effect on your brain activity, as research has shown. I joke with people that, as an entrepreneur with an unpredictable and often hectic schedule, I need to read to power down, but I also read to power up. Reading aids in stress management, especially when you feel prepared by keeping up with current events and best practices. My library card and Kindle app have gotten much use since I became an entrepreneur!

As I stated previously, reading has become fashionable again thanks to the Harry Potter books and to social media sites. Countless people access social media every day, at any time of day. That includes Facebook, Google+, Twitter, Tumblr, WordPress, and other blogs. In addition, the ease of communicating via e-mail and of quickly creating your own website without outsourcing the task (which we used to do and have to pay good money for, too!) has become a motivator for our children to achieve literacy.

But what about the busy entrepreneur, trying to juggle personal and professional responsibilities? Trying to make the most of time spent at the office and then with the family at home? That time crunch is why I advocate that entrepreneurs begin using the iPad for everyday tasks. Start small — reading, browsing the web, answering e-mails, and looking at photos. The iPad is a weapon in your arsenal. Reading an e-book or saved web article becomes much more feasible when you can do it on a mobile device. Women tell me that they read more now on their mobile devices in between juggling everything else in their busy schedules. Technology has made it possible for more readers to find the time to read — on their commute to work, while waiting in the doctor's office or in the airport, when sitting on a plane, or standing in line at the grocery or mall. Just make sure to stay mindful of your surroundings and be safe. Also, be aware of what the kids are up to when they think you're not looking!

Seriously, the beauty of reading, especially on an iPad, lies in the fact that you can break up your reading to match your routine. Even if you leave it and go do something else, your place is kept, and you can pick up where you left off, seamlessly and effortlessly. Which brings me to my next point. The first books for an entrepreneur to read are obviously those that will help you promote your product or service. Since that sort of bibliography is reserved for the Appendix, let me instead suggest books for your reading list to help you increase your tech IQ with an iPad. Let me suggest several books that I recommend in my Socially Speaking™ iPad Basics Bootcamp Seminars. They are handpicked for the busy entrepreneur who has limited time to learn the practical applications of the iPad.

Penina's Pointers

Reading List: iPad Manuals

Biersdorfer, J. D. (2013). *iPad: The Missing Manual.* Sebastopol, California: O'Reilly Media.

Carlson, Jeff (2013). *The iPad Air and the iPad Mini Pocket Guide, Fifth Edition.* Berkeley, California: Peach Pit Press.

Feiler, Jesse (2012). *iWork for Dummies, Second Edition.* Hoboken, New Jersey: John Wiley & Sons.

Fleishman, Glenn (2012). *Five Star Apps: The Best iPhone and iPad Apps for Work and Play.* Berkeley, California: Peach Pit Press.

Hess, Alan (2012). *The New iPad Fully Loaded.* Indianapolis: John Wiley & Sons.

Meyers, Peter (2011). *Best iPad Apps: The Guide for Discriminating Downloaders.* Sebastopol, California: O'Reilly Media.

Negrino, Tom (2012). *iCloud: Visual Quick Start Guide.* Berkeley, California: Peach Pit Press.

Rosenzweig, Gary (2013). *My iPad, 6th Edition.* Indianapolis: Pearson Education/Que Publishing.

Rich, Jason R. (2012). *Your iPad At Work.* Indianapolis: Pearson Education/Que Publishing.

Rich, Jason R. (2012). *How to Do Everything iCloud.* New York: McGraw Hill.

Rich, Jason R. (2013). *iPad and iPhone: Tips & Tricks — Covers iOS 7.* Indianapolis: Pearson Education/Que Publishing.

Sparks, David (2011). *iPad At Work.* Hoboken, New Jersey: John Wiley & Sons.

Wang, Wallace (2012). *My New iPad: A User's Guide, Third Edition.* San Francisco: No Starch Press.

Watson, Lonzell (2011). *Teach Yourself Visually: The New iPad.* Indianapolis: John Wiley & Sons.

FOUR

Nuts & Bolts

E = ENTREPRENEURSHIP

FYI: Entrepreneurship Is Not Just a Male Domain

KEY WEBSITES

- http://bit.ly/entrepreneurial-expectancies-of-women
- http://bit.ly/women-entrepreneur-behavior
- http://bit.ly/childrens-beliefs-about-entrepreneurship
- http://bit.ly/peter-drucker-on-leadership
- http://bit.ly/entrepreneurship-the-new-womens-movement
- http://bit.ly/why-female-entrepreneurs-need-mentors
- http://bit.ly/are-you-ready-to-be-the-boss
- http://bit.ly/innovation-in-other-half-of-economy

Quotes to Ponder

I was motivated simply because I didn't want a boss.

— Barbara Corcoran

In the business world, the rearview mirror is always clearer than the windshield.

— Warren Buffet

Definition

Entrepreneur: One who organizes, manages, and assumes the risks of a business or enterprise.

— *The Merriam-Webster Dictionary*

I N THIS BOOK I've spoken about an entrepreneur's inner landscape and how it affects both the mindset and skill set that you need to hone — to make a hook, woo clients, and approach a venture. Now, however, I'll go back in time a bit and touch on the changing business landscape of the past few years. I'll briefly highlight how it affected the rapid increase of entrepreneurial pursuits worldwide.

Entrepreneurship has been in lock-step with capitalism for centuries, so why is it currently being heralded as the new frontier, especially in the United States? Do a web search, or even search LinkedIn, and you'll see a myriad of articles about entrepreneurship. Check out Guy Kawasaki (former Macintosh evangelist and prolific writer) and Sir Richard Branson (the unorthodox founder of the Virgin Group), both of whom are part of my regular content curation process and considered pioneers in thought leadership circles. I personally like to read what they're saying on LinkedIn, on Twitter (https://twitter.com/richardbranson), and on this interesting website of curated content by Guy Kawasaki, Alltop.com (http://alltop.com).

Curating Content

There are several ways for you to curate content — creating your own personalized news magazine by streaming articles to an entire section you can devote to entrepreneurship. I use Zite and have it synced across all my iOS devices, and I try to read it regularly, even if I just read the top featured stories. I also recommend regularly perusing Google+ and SlideShare and even creating and uploading your own slideshows to share with others. For practical advice about content curation that is timely, relevant, and worth blogging about to your social media followers, I recommend perusing these links:

- http://bit.ly/get-real-with-relevance
- http://bit.ly/screw-sexy-be-helpful
- http://bit.ly/your-content-has-a-shelf-life

Check out other online sources such as Feedly, Newsify, Slate, Digg, Pulse, Flipboard, and my favorite, Zite. For best practices on entrepreneurship check out under30CEO.com, Forbes.com, or *Forbes, Entrepreneur,* or *Inc.* magazines. The public appetite for practical, historical, psychological, and financial information — tidbits, quotes, articles, and strategies — has reached an all-time high.

Why is entrepreneurship so popular? Because as Robert Kiyosaki, author of the enlightening book *Rich Dad, Poor Dad,* says, "When times are bad is when the real entrepreneurs emerge." America is slowly getting back on its economic feet, climbing out of the bottom of the proverbial well and picking up the pieces of Humpty Dumpty (Wall Street) and moving on. I'm referring, of course, to the Great Recession, which began in December 2007 according to the National Bureau of Economic Research.

In an informative article written by Scott Shane in March 2011, "The Great Recession's Effect on Entrepreneurship" (http://bit.ly/great-recessions-effect-on-entrepreneurship), data was presented from a study by the Ewing Marion Kauffman Foundation that showed that the highest rise of entrepreneurship in decades occurred in 2009 (incidentally the same year I started my own journey as an entrepreneur). Patterns. Seemingly unrelated events but actually parts of a pattern. Despite Kiyosaki's claim that entrepreneurs emerge when times are bad, Professor Shane concludes that "by most available measures, the Great Recession's effect on entrepreneurship was negative." He believes that this was due to a decrease in self-employed individuals and the formation of new businesses. But it's crucial to note his geographical location at the time he wrote and published his article (Ohio, which was hard hit).

Interestingly enough his findings were both endorsed and disputed two months later, in May 2011, when Robert Fairlie, literally across the country in the Department of Economics at the University of California Santa Cruz, published a paper entitled "Entrepreneurship, Economic Conditions, and the Great Recession" (http://bit.ly/entrepreneurship-economics-great-recession). In that paper Fairlie writes, "I can predict the entire increase in entrepreneurship rates in the past few years from only the rapidly deteriorating labor market conditions. Estimates for home ownership and housing equity, on the other hand, indicate a small *decline* in entrepreneurship since the start of the recession. Although a large number of small businesses struggled and failed in the Great Recession, many new businesses that ultimately will be very successful may have been created." Again it's crucial again to note this author's geographical and philosophical location at the time this paper was submitted and published (University of California Santa Cruz).

I believe it's telling that the Fairlie paper came out of the same general location as one of the U.S.'s entrepreneurial tech hubs —Silicon Valley. It gives you different data from a different sample and therefore a different impression from Shane's findings in the midwest. Note that Shane's article was written in landlocked, less-tech-oriented Ohio (at that time), whose closer proximity to the auto industry debacle in Detroit makes for more pessimistic findings. Shane went on to write another disquieting article in *Small Business Trends* on 19 August 2013, "Few Americans Invest in Startups" (http://bit.ly/few-americans-invest-in-startups). He writes, "Few American households hold equity investments in private businesses operated by someone else. The share of Americans who make informal investments — investments in private businesses belonging to friends, families and strangers — has changed little in recent years. Moreover, the typical amount invested by those providing funds was only $5,000." I find the data and article interesting and worth reading in its entirety.

Most interesting is the July 2012 article published by the University of Missouri's News Bureau, "Economic Recession Leads to Increased Entrepreneurship" (http://bit.ly/recession-increases-entrepreneurship). In this article Maria Figueroa-Armijos, a doctoral candidate at the university's Truman School of Public Affairs, is quoted as saying that the Great Recession has spurred a trend where "there is much more economic support for opportunity entrepreneurs than for people starting their own businesses out of necessity."

The article cites two types of entrepreneurship: opportunity and necessity, which we'll cover in more detail later. It also reports findings from a study published in the *Entrepreneurship Research Journal* about the significance of the type of entrepreneurship and the geographical location (*urban* or *rural*) on the growth of entreneurship. According to Figueroa-Armijos, the findings were profound. "These findings offer policy makers an opportunity to permanently increase entrepreneurial involvement of historically under-represented groups. Considering the decline of rural populations, rural development strategies must be re-examined. Increased support for necessity-driven self-employment not only offers a way of improving the incomes of rural residents, but also provides an opportunity to create more overall entrepreneurial activity following the recession."

Why am I citing these three articles? Why is it crucial to note both the type of entrepreneurship and the location where one practices it? Because taking into account both factors will play a crucial role in determining the success of your endeavors to promote change. Just as costumes and scenery (setting the stage) play a huge role in the success of a play, learning the topography of this new frontier, the lay of the land, helps you to more methodically and accurately chart your entrepreneurial course at its inception.

What do the two types of entrepreneurship really mean for women? As stated previously, the two types of entrepreneurship are opportunity and necessity. The latter is usually a result of pay cuts, downsizing, outsourcing, and hard economic times — things we all saw happen on the home front and then abroad these past few years. Entrepreneurship by necessity fosters short-term solutions and linear thinking about the present. It tends to affect your immediate locale and how you manage financially with the resources at hand. Opportunity entrepreneurship, however, results from a rise in long-term, more radical, unconventional, outside-the-box thinking, which tends to have a ripple effect that may not be felt right away. Economists call this effect *disruptive innovation*.

Disruptive innovation is a term coined by businessman and Harvard professor Clayton Christensen in his 1997 book, *The Innovator's Dilemma*. According to Christenson, "An innovation that is disruptive allows a whole new population of consumers at the bottom of a market access to a product or service that was historically only accessible to consumers with a lot of money or a lot of skill." Like the smartphone. Like the Kindle. Like the iPad. Like Tim Kring taking his *Heroes* story to the masses via the Internet.

There are two arenas where disruptive innovation has really been felt in the past decade: the technology arena, especially with the release of the iPhone in 2007, and the education arena, especially with the No Child Left Behind Law enacted by former president George W. Bush in 2002. The implications of these disruptive innovations are that women, now more than ever, are in a novel position to effectively, profitably, and successfully join the Entrepreneurial Revolution. Due to the decreasing ruralization of the United States, in particular, and the increasing societal freedoms women experience (their widespread ability to travel, live independently, and learn, use, and implement mobile technology, particularly social media), it's now much easier to more meaningfully, and profitably, become an entrepreneur. This is especially true for female entrepreneurs in the education arena, the technology arena, or both.

Obviously, given my background, these two arenas are of interest to me. But the healthcare arena — public service and civil institutions — can also be mined for opportunities for disruptive innovation. As far back as three decades ago, economists and business leaders were already calling for reforms in education and healthcare. Peter Drucker, one of the foremost experts on entrepreneurship and author of the 1985 classic, *Innovation and Entrepreneurship*, was concerned about education and healthcare. He asked, "Why is innovation in the public-service institution so important?" His answer was that public-service institutions have become too big and too important in developed countries. Building entrepreneurial management into existing public-service institutions may be the foremost political task of this generation. Prophetic words. Inspiring words. A call to arms, starting so many years ago. Words that have lingered, as has his profound legacy since his passing in 2005.

A year before Drucker published his seminal work (which still remains required reading in economic circles today), a research study was published that investigated whether entrepreneurship was perceived to be a male domain. In 1984, *Sex Roles Journal of Research* published an article by Marilyn Kourilsky and Michael Campbell based on the research, "Sex Differences in a Simulated Classroom Economy: Children's Beliefs about Entrepreneurship."

The findings indicated that after 938 children in the third to sixth grades took a crash course in entrepreneurship (risk-taking, economic success, and persistence) they no longer felt that entrepreneurship was a male domain.

In the past year, especially, more women have been inducted into the ranks of entrepreneurship. In fact, more people overall are being encouraged to become entrepreneurs. Or maybe they're being discouraged from accepting the status quo at their old jobs or entry-level positions offered to newly hired graduates. Two articles that caught my attention seem to share the idea that entrepreneurship is fast becoming an expected way of life, especially for the millennial generation. In late September 2013, Andrea Huspeni wrote an article for *Entrepreneur* magazine entitled "Millennials are Snubbing the Corporate World for Entrepreneurship." In it she provides an infographic that shows the reasons that millennials are pursuing a different path: "The number 1 reason is freedom, followed by ability to choose projects and unlimited income potential."

One month later Anthony Dejolde wrote an article for *Lifehack* entitled, "Why Everyone Needs to Become An Entrepreneur" (http://bit.ly/become-an-entrepreneur). In the article he provided an infographic and an explanation. Economic shifts and new healthcare trends are rapidly changing the way companies hire and retain employees. "Now everyone, that includes you, have to turn entrepreneur just to preserve a job. To explain further, freelancers, contractors, and freelance consultants have lower rates compared to full-time workers with benefits."

The Entrepreneurial Revolution is currently underway but seems to be moving at a slower pace than anticipated. Rieva Lesonsky, Founder and CEO of GrowBiz Media, wrote an article on 25 October 2013 entitled, "Why Aren't Women-Owned Businesses Growing Faster?" (http://bit.ly/growing-faster). In it she quotes Betsy Myers, Founding Director of the Center for Women in Business at Bentley University and former head of the U.S. Office of Women's

Business Ownership. "Myers thinks a transformation is about to happen — courtesy of millennials, who will make up 47 percent of the workforce next year. Myers also suspects part of the issue is 'men define themselves by their careers; women don't.' That, she says, will change as millennials, who want a more balanced life, join the workforce." I agree.

I was also interviewed for this eye-opening article and provided a quote too. "Women still lag behind men because our access to funding and technology training has been hampered by the still-skewed work/life balance we attempt and the gender-specific roles we are often expected to step into." I believe that there's also a third reason that female entrepreneurship is a slowly growing movement. In the 90s, when female entrepreneurship began to emerge as a viable option, the overall technological infrastructure to sustain it was too new, and that detracted from job security. Job security was (and continues to be) a real concern for many women juggling work and family obligations. Also, the 90s saw a resurgence in women's pursuit of jobs in the healthcare and special educational sectors due to advances in medicine, ground-breaking research findings in autism and other developmental disabilities, and the overall ease of obtaining government loans or scholarships for pursuing degrees in these fields of study. But the Great Recession taught us that job security is tenuous in all workplace settings and arenas and no longer a reason to avoid becoming an entrepreneur. This economic reality as well as technological advances that provide the infrastructure needed to sustain female entrepreneurship have made the pursuit of female entrepreneurship more popular and attainable these days.

In July 2013 Megan Totka wrote an article for the Business 2 Community Forum entitled, "Why Now is a Great Time to be a Female Entrepreneur" (http://bit.ly/its-a-great-time). She cites incentives ranging from flexible hours to home office options as well as creative collaboration in app development as reasons that it's a great time. As an app developer and someone who initially started my business working from home, I couldn't agree more. I just wish more women outside corporate and tech settings would heed the advice and join the Entrepreneurial Revolution.

It's time to induct more women from the education and health-care arenas. A second call to arms has recently been sounded. It was sounded in May 2013 by an unexpected source. The fact that the source was unexpected makes it that much more important to heed. That source, Evan Burfield, is an erudite, cutting-edge thinker and writer. He has been an entrepreneur since graduating from high school. He won the Webb Medley economics prize for his thesis at Oxford. He's the co-founder of 1776, an incubator platform based in Washington, DC.

In May 2013 Burfield published an article about entrepreneurship entitled, "Innovation in the Other Half of the Economy" (http://bit.ly/innovation-in-other-half-of-economy) for the Tech & Innovation/Perspectives column on the Ideas Lab website. In it he argues, "Education, health, energy, transportation, and government services are massive markets trapped in the industrial era — rife with exciting opportunities for entrepreneurial transformation." He posits that the standard business models in these arenas must undergo radical changes, which will positively and paradoxically effect both consumer stagnation and consumer renovation. He hopes that his company, 1776, through practicing new-age entrepreneurship involving mentoring and liquid seed capital, will help effect the necessary financial and historic changes needed in society today.

Burfield's article resonated with me, especially his final observation, which made me actually post a comment on the Ideas Lab site. He writes, "It's profound, however, when an entrepreneur changes the arc of history by improving the way we educate our children, our health, or how we manage our resources." I commented as follows: "Your sentiment echoes mine. As a pediatric speech therapist/Autism Specialist, turned Educational Technology Consultant/Entrepreneur, my goal has been to educate our educators to join the

Tech Revolution, and integrate toys and tech to teach social skills to children, particular young preschoolers with Autism. I started my boutique educational seminar company in 2010, with a simple message: learn to bridge the gap between a special child's readiness to learn and actual performance. I saw early on, that someone had to come forward, and evangelize the iPad as a game changer in the world of special education. I launched my Socially Speaking™ App for iPad in May 2012, and my Socially Speaking™ iPad Seminar in October 2012. My social skills curriculum and App are being used all over the USA, Canada, and soon in Zambia, Africa at the CLASP International Autism Clinic. My next project is to empower women in the educational sector to join the Entrepreneurial Revolution. It's time for more of us to change the arc of history, one child at a time."

As the saying goes, "Them's fighting words!" The article eloquently and succinctly delivers the formula for female entrepreneurs to keep in mind when pursuing their own ventures: to provide services or products that will produce disruptive innovation. Fortunately many women who historically, organically, and biologically have already veered into healthcare and educational professions have already positioned themselves for economic innovation through entrepreneurship.

I've given you food for thought on *why* women are poised to become the new wave of competent entrepreneurs. Let me first do a round-up; then I'll move on to *how* you'll accomplish this.

Penina's Pointers
Strategies for Positioning Yourself to Ride the Wave

⊛ **Get informed.** Learn about economic and technological trends affecting your industry (Zite iOS app, follow the news, Coursera.com, online newsletters, industry conferences and trade shows, TED talks, etc.). Also consider taking an online course — a MOOC (massive open online course) from Coursera.org, Udacity.com, or Udemy.com, just to name three sources on my radar.

⊛ **Get educated.** Not sure you have the ability or knowledge you need to telecommute? Learn about what entrepreneurship advantages and disadvantages exist in your geographical location. There are newly penned articles out there such as this one by Nanette Fondas in *The Atlantic* on 19 July 2013, "How Men and Women Use Flexible Work Policies Differently" (http://bit.ly/flexible-work-policies). There are also infographics about this topic going viral online every week, such as this one from 3 May 2013, on Intuit's small business blog: http://bit.ly/top-cities-for-female-entrepreneurs.

⊛ **Get moving.** Let your voice be heard, either in real time by giving a presentation on your area of expertise, or online by carefully commenting on relevant articles that gain a lot of web traffic. Choose wisely. Link those articles and comments to your website, and post about them on your other social media sites.

Successful Entrepreneurship 101: In a Nutshell

KEY WEBSITES

- http://bit.ly/what-first-time-entrepreneurs-should-know
- http://bit.ly/start-up-strategy
- http://bit.ly/10-lessons-from-startup-entrepreneur
- http://bit.ly/drucker-12-keys-to-success
- http://bit.ly/choose-a-niche-to-lead
- http://bit.ly/how-you-run-your-startup
- http://bit.ly/einstein-inspired-tactics-for-marketers
- http://bit.ly/think-like-a-dolphin-not-a-shark
- http://bit.ly/what-you-need-to-know-about-branding
- http://bit.ly/10-tips-to-stay-on-track
- http://bit.ly/ways-to-use-pinterest-for-business
- http://bit.ly/pitch-your-startup-in-3-minutes
- http://bit.ly/what-would-steve-jobs-do
- http://bit.ly/7-entrepreneur-lessons-from-cooking
- http://bit.ly/12-ways-to-spy-on-competitors
- http://bit.ly/e-myth-revisited-summary
- http://bit.ly/do-not-take-venture-capital
- http://bit.ly/7-questions-to-answer
- http://bit.ly/ways-entrepreneurs-lie-to-themselves
- http://bit.ly/lessons-women-can-teach-each-other
- http://bit.ly/dont-wait-for-an-invitation
- http://bit.ly/you-dont-need-to-be-all-powerful

- http://bit.ly/skip-outside-investors
- http://bit.ly/how-to-hang-tough
- http://bit.ly/dangerous-lies-entrepreneurs-tell-themselves
- http://bit.ly/be-a-successful-startup-founder
- http://bit.ly/launching-your-dream-business
- http://bit.ly/the-zuckerberg-effect
- http://bit.ly/entrepreneurship-according-to-drucker
- http://bit.ly/relationships-matter
- http://bit.ly/self-promotion-drives-success
- http://bit.ly/harvey-mackay-advice-for-entrepreneurs
- http://bit.ly/entrepreneur-conference-lessons
- http://bit.ly/what-successful-entrepreneurs-have-in-common
- http://bit.ly/social-media-obsession

Quotes to Ponder

Success is like reaching an important birthday and finding you're exactly the same.

— Audrey Hepburn

There are no secrets to success. It is the result of hard work, preparation, and learning from failure.

— Colin Powell

Definition

Success: A favorable or desired outcome. The attainment of wealth, favor, or eminence.

— *The Merriam-Webster Dictionary*

THIS SECTION of the book has been one of the most difficult for me to organize and write. I've spent so much time on research and drafts only to realize that I was providing conflicting information, too much information, or too little practical information. In analyzing my notes, my research, my cache of books (many borrowed from my local library) and articles (many found online) that I saved to my Evernote and Pocket apps, I found patterns. Patterns that jogged my memory, my episodic memory of my own unfolding, continuing, unexpected journey as an entrepreneur. I've therefore decided that this section of the book should provide true survival guide tips for a successful female entrepreneur, broken down into three categories. Any more and the message would become a series of circumlocutions, which I abhor as both an avid reader and professional educator and public speaker.

So there are three areas in which to hone your entrepreneurial competency in order to achieve success and to orchestrate change:

1. **Creative input:** Put your theory of mind (perspective, inner landscape) to use, finding economic and societal patterns in events and outcomes and connect the two patterns using your strengths, knowledge, outside-the-box thinking, and strategies for implementation or revision of your mission.

2. **Passionate output:** Use public forums, social media, word of mouth, trade magazines, industry conferences, and fellow passionate members of your ecosystem who are on board to spread the word about your mission.

3. **Timing:** Time the trajectory of execution and expansion of your mission. Develop a system of checks and balances using your time management skills and instincts, economic forecasts, and advice from valued, proven mentors, about when to forge ahead and when to stay still. To put it another way, tweak your timing regarding when to bootstrap, when to accept venture capital, when to trust your gut and

take that leap of faith, and when to seek mentorship. Walk a tightrope between multitasking and laser focus on the things you need to do in order to do what you do.

Creative Input

REMEMBER the Febreze fabric deodorizer TV commercials? There's one I like, in particular, where a blindfolded man, sitting on a dirty, falling-apart couch sprayed with a specific Febreze scent, breathes deeply and declares, "It smells like children's blankets." His perspective has been hampered by his decreased sense of vision. But his heightened olfactory sense, which connected to his memories of being a father, causes him to make that declaration. Your past episodic memories, combined with your present perceptions about the surrounding world (based on input, or lack thereof, from your five senses) are what you need to use your theory of mind successfully to color outside the lines. You need those memories and perceptions to observe patterns and infer outcomes of events you experience or actions you take yourself or with others.

These two neuro-cognitive processes, observation and inferencing, are necessary to effectively navigate your environment. It's especially true for entrepreneurs. The very climate we immerse ourselves in requires us to make small, on-the-fly mental adjustments in behavior, because we're analyzing and categorizing the behavior of others and projecting how this behavior will affect events or outcomes. (Life is all about The Butterfly Effect, where small changes can have large effects. Seeing patterns.)

The road to successful entrepreneurship starts with becoming educated, an observer of human nature, which results in the enrichment of your actions — the ones executed in hidden increments, and the ones executed publicly on a grand scale. It then continues with the behavioral implementation of specific entrepreneurial skills. These skills are needed to implement four strategies for becoming a successful entrepreneur.

These strategies were first proposed by Peter Drucker, dubbed the Father of Modern Management, who saw entrepreneurship as a behavior instead of a personality trait. In *Innovation and Entrepreneurship*, he lists the four entrepreneurial strategies that are needed for successful entrepreneurship:

1. Being "fustest with the mostest"
2. "Hitting them where they ain't"
3. Finding and occupying a specialized ecological niche
4. Changing the economic characteristics of a product, market, or industry

Drucker argues that true, insightful, and competent entrepreneurs position themselves physically, philosophically, or both, to cause change. To do so by being the key suppliers of specific services or products in niche markets that, over time, essentially cause changes in the way people live and work and cause reform in public service industries. This change is what Clayton Christenson later referred to as disruptive innovation in *The Innovator's Dilemma*. I recommend that you delve further into both compelling books for further information.

Seth Godin, another great thinker, entrepreneur extraordinaire, and prolific writer, author of the 1998 bestseller, *The Bootstrapper's Bible,* also writes about entrepreneurial strategy. He states that entrepreneurs need to have publicized manifestoes about how to live and conduct themselves while increasing entrepreneurial competency. One of his affirmations stated in his manifesto is, "I am a laser beam. Opportunities will try to cloud my focus, but I will not waver from my stated goal and plan — until I change it. And I know that plans were meant to be changed."

His book is a treasure trove of practical wisdom that all current and future entrepreneurs are encouraged to read. What's important to note, though, is that the necessity of adapting to change, as well as creative thinking, are built into his manifesto — the Godin Directive. It's also important to note the implication that bootstrapping is a feasible option for a startup looking to stay afloat, while engaging in some unconventional problem solving and behaviors to avoid using venture capital. I was quite reluctant to raise outside funds when starting my business, so I've been meticulously following Godin's advice, as well as other proven voices and methods.

I highly recommend that you read and follow others who exhibit out-of-the-box thinking. Look for that quality when seeking mentors and project collaborators. Look for entrepreneurial articles showcasing this trait, like those of Seth Godin. Another person you should check out is Dudley Lynch, author of *LEAP! How to Think Like a Dolphin & Do the Next Right, Smart Thing Come Hell or High Water*. I found this 12 June 2013, article on under30ceo.com about his book very enlightening, and I hope you will too: http://bit.ly/think-like-a-dolphin-not-a-shark.

Passionate Output

I'VE STATED IT BEFORE and will do so again: Honing your social media technology savvy and public speaking skills is crucial to being a successful entrepreneur. So is protecting your digital reputation — content, media, testimonials, and timeline. How do you do it? By being direct, passionate, and compassionate about your mission, your cause, and your raison d'être for providing your service or product. Go to seminars or trade shows in your industry, as both a listener and a speaker. Contribute articles, meaningful strategies, and practical news to your base, pro bono. Incorporate themes when posting on social media so that you ensure cohesiveness and easier reading and so your passion gets demonstrated repeatedly. Build rapport through shared goals and interests with people in your microcosm to help you get your message out there. Share stories — about yourself and about others.

Storytelling is an age-old educational and newly re-purposed digital marketing technique that's been "rediscovered" by social media and communications management gurus and thought leaders. It's been written about extensively lately and was one of the running themes at the Hubspot Inbound 2013 marketing convention in Boston in August. I had the pleasure of attending for the first time and heard inspiring talks on this subject from the likes of Seth Godin, Pamela Slim (whose take on it will be published in her upcoming book, *Body of Work*), and Dan Lyons (journalist and author of the very clever blog series *The Secret Diary of Steve Jobs*). I paid particular attention to Dan Lyons' talk about the importance of storytelling in marketing as a means of providing media representations and lessons (mentorship) about humanity and archetypes. He discussed archetypal storytelling and marketing, using Steve Jobs as an example.

What was so great about the way Steve Jobs told a story?

⊛ He used emotive words to tell the tale

⊛ He gave an exaggerated and hyperbolized accounting of what's happening

⊛ He was one of the first to practice psychological transparency (Lesson: Dare to be human. Speak to a larger truth by being yourself.)

⊛ He used all the elemental archetypes of a story:

- Betrayal, disillusionment, or need by a protagonist starts the personal quest

- Identification of the underdog, so we know who to root for when the challenges start piling up

- Revenge arc — the hero returns to turn the tables on the naysayers or enemies

- Turnaround, resolution of conflict

Everyone loves a good story. Stories are important because they provide patterns of a life lived and patterns to embrace or reject, depending on the outcome. Stories give us concrete examples of a sequence of events, a way of problem solving, and a blueprint of a script for you to follow or deviate from when embarking on your own script. Whether on a quest for truth, justice, or the American Dream, chances are there's a story for that embedded in a book, movie, TV show, or video game app.

I confess I'm not into sports or gaming, yet I love sports movies (*Remember the Titans, The Rookie*) and used to love *Myst* and *The Sims*. Why? Because the elemental archetypes of any story boil down to one theme: causality. The seesaw upon which action/reaction and good/evil are balanced. A great story arc involves and depicts the hero's struggle to orchestrate change, for himself or herself or for others, by finding new ways to work and invoke archetypes, lessons, and the causality loop that life is based on. How someone uses what life has thrown him or her to effect change makes for a hero, an archetype, and makes for riveting reading. Think of the complex multilayered story lines Shonda Rhimes creates for her hallmark, award-winning TV shows *Grey's Anatomy* and *Scandal.* Think of the nuanced, insightful story lines Michelle King creates with her husband Robert King for the award-winning, critically acclaimed TV show *The Good Wife.* Think of the worlds of Buffy and Angel, created by master storyteller Joss Whedon. Think of the TV show *Heroes,* created by master visual digitalization guru Tim Kring. The causality loop being reconfigured so that a linear trajectory is not always the outcome, let alone the desired path.

Archetypal storytelling and consulting for branding and marketing purposes has since become a hot topic and legitimate avenue of entrepreneurship, as seen from Diane Bertolin's fall 2013 blog series *Archetypal Consulting* and her subsequent e-book for Hubspot on this subject. I recommend that everyone read her blogposts — educators, entrepreneurs, marketers, public speakers, and those trying to forge a human connection with others through dating, marriage, and all the steps in between. They are insightful analyses of the human condition, seen through the eyes of a female business woman and social media marketing expert.

Harnessing the power of storytelling, of identifying archetypes, and implementing that knowledge, together with your resiliency, will help you transition from *me* to *we*, especially when it comes to entrepreneurship and marketing yourself in terms of your service or product. It enables you to learn from others, empathize with them, and become more flexible and adaptive when your own story changes and/or intersects with another's. These traits need to be honed individually and fostered collectively — at home, in public, and at work. How do you do it? By understanding archetypes and the impact of hearing and internalizing stories (http://bit.ly/use-archetypes-to-create-your-brand).

When planning on honing your storytelling to improve both the delivery and the content of your message, you should read *Made to Stick* by Chip and Dan Heath. In it they list six principles for effectively getting your message across.

The Six Principles of Sticky Ideas, Proposed by the Heath Brothers and Interpreted by Penina

1. **Simplicity:** Find the core of your intent and translate that verbally and in writing as your mission and vision statements, and present these statements publicly, including via social media.

2. **Unexpectedness:** Find what would naturally block your message from getting out there and solve that problem technologically or intellectually or both.

3. **Concreteness:** Break down your business plan methodically and implement it over time at pre-planned, key intervals for more effective delivery of your service or product with less financial risk.

4. **Credibility:** Get people to agree with, believe in, and endorse your service or product publicly. Nurture your real-time relationships and protect your digital reputation while doing so.

5. **Emotions:** Get people to identify with and share your vision by showing that you care and that your service or product really addresses a particular problem. Emote!

6. **Stories:** Inspire others to act based on your examples and tales. Learn public speaking skills and brush up on your presentation delivery — content and style.

When planning to incorporate stories into your message, you should take a look at the story and character development of the TV show *Touch* for inspiration. Tim Kring encompasses all the thematic elements found in a story that sticks. So does Joss Whedon in his televised series *Buffy the Vampire Slayer*. Both men are master storytellers; you can learn much from them. I certainly did.

According to the Heath brothers, there are three types of universal themes in stories. Taken from *Made to Stick*, I've listed them below, along with practical examples of the three main character archetypes, using well-known films to make my points:

⚙ **Challenge plot:** Overcoming obstacles (Jennifer Lawrence as Katniss Everdeen in *The Hunger Games*; Sarah Michelle Geller as Buffy Summers in *Buffy the Vampire Slayer*; Diane Lane as Frances Mayes in *Under the Tuscan Sun*; Will Smith as Del Spooner in *I, Robot*; Dennis Quaid as Jimmy Morris in *The Rookie*; and Tom Hanks as the title character in *Forrest Gump*)

⚙ **Connection plot:** Unexpected friendships or relationships (Emma Stone as Skeeter and Viola Davis as Aibileen Clark in *The Help*; Sandra Bullock as Leigh Ann Tuohy and Quinton Aaron as Michael Oher in *The Blind Side*; Angela Bassett as Stella Payne and Taye Diggs as Winston Shakespeare in *How Stella Got Her Groove Back*; Sanaa Lathan as Kenya McQueen and Simon Baker as Brian Kelly in *Something New*; and Tom Cruise as Captain Nathan Algren and Ken Watanabe as Katsumoto in *The Last Samurai*)

⊛ **Creativity plot:** Inspired people doing inspiring things (Whoopi Goldberg as Celie Johnson in *The Color Purple*; Mulan in Disney's *Mulan*; Winona Ryder as Jo March in *Little Women*; Jodi Foster as Dr. Ellie Arroway in *Contact*; Cuba Gooding Jr. as Carl Brashear in *Men of Honor*; and Daniel Craig as Tuvia Bielski in *Defiance*)

According to an October 2012 interview given by Tim Kring (http://bit.ly/future-of-storytelling), his Conspiracy For Good Project came about because of stories — stories that began as web-based fan fiction about *Heroes* and then included real world players to orchestrate change.

Kring believes that, ultimately, stories are always inspirational because they have "the ability to connect one another, to let people know one another, to share and allow for an incredibly exciting movement to rise up around various ideas." In the interview the narrator gives the example of a musician named Nadira X who tries to build a children's library in Zambia. She has a whopper of a story to share. A true one. An entrepreneurial one. An inspiring one.

Nadira tries to instigate change and comes up against seemingly insurmountable odds and corporate greed. She discovers that Blackwell Briggs, a British company, tries to interfere with construction of the library. She finds proof that the company committed fraud to further its agenda about an oil pipeline. The conspiracy is exposed by her and fellow members of that project who help her in her quest. On the world stage. On the Internet. Riveting stuff. Both Kring's words and the entire ten minute video. Worth checking out and sharing with others.

Entrepreneurial competence requires that the message sticks. It thus involves:

⊛ Effective delivery of the message sharing the mission

⊛ Effective leadership in implementing the nuts and bolts of the mission and seeing the process to fruition

Chip and Dan Heath provide an excellent resource for effective leadership and delivery implementation. I endorse their book as well as those by Seth Godin. Godin's pithy, deceptively simple book, *Tribes,* also gives practical insight and easy-to-understand information about effective leadership. He has a unique way of seeing things that will make you think. Read his books and blogs and see how your thinking changes.

In *Tribes,* Godin defines a tribe as "any group of people, large or small, who are connected to one another, a leader, and idea. It's [in] our nature [to join]. The Internet has eliminated the barriers of geography, cost, and time." He asks and answers this question:

Q: Who is going to lead these tribes?

A: You are. "Great leaders create movements by empowering the tribe to communicate. They establish the foundation for people to make connections, as opposed to commanding people to follow them."

He then goes on to describe what leadership really means, which can be summed up by three telling quotes:

⊛ "Leaders figure out how to step into those vacuums and create motion. They work hard to generate movement — the sort of movement that can transform a group into a tribe."

⊛ "Not only aren't leaders most people, but the members of the most important tribes aren't most people either."

⊛ "Every leader cares for and supports a movement. What marketers and organizers and people who care are discovering is that they can ignite a micro-movement and then be propelled by the people who choose to follow it."

Godin raises many interesting questions in *Tribes,* including: How does a leader maximize tribe effectiveness and build on the passion and belief in his or her mission? Let me paraphrase the answers. A leader:

⊛ Turns collective passion or outlook into a cause that matters — with joint goals to effect change

⊛ Promotes a communication paradigm, lingo, and forum to plan the tribe's goals and share info

⊛ Becomes an evangelist about the mission to expand the tribe

Godin's shared wisdom can be found in *Linchpin* as well. I read both. So should you. You can find resources — books, articles, websites — on the subject of leadership in the appendices at the end of this book.

How to Increase Your Passionate Output to Create a Movement

BELOW IS A BLUEPRINT about passionate output for female entrepreneurs to follow based on what I've read and from my own experience. The blueprint is divided into two sections, leadership homework and leadership principles.

Leadership Homework

⊛ **Promote your cause.** Publish a mission statement to be shared with others, in real time and online.

⊛ **Publicize your ability to be a solution to a problem.** Establish a digital footprint via social media and list your contact info. Be accessible.

⊛ **Connect with your tribe.** Create a website. Find public speaking engagements. Write comments on articles online, in your field or on topics of interest, and go to conferences and meetings. Use social media to attract followers.

⊛ **Maintain momentum.** Movements take time and patience. They cost money. Don't quit your day job and hit the gas pedal, yet. Try to bootstrap for as long as you can.

⊛ **Methodically expand your movement.** Create opportunities and forums for your followers to contribute and be heard. Analyze patterns, seeing where to step in. That's what this book is all about.

Leadership Principles

⊛ **Practice fairness and transparency.** Be nice and sincere, on and off the court. Keep your word. Be honest. Share the glory. Admit errors.

⊛ **Make the movement bigger than you.** Your service or product should enable others to get informed about how to effect change in their milieu. Remember the saying, "Teach the man to fish ..."

⊛ **Help your movement thrive by growing.** Methodical time management, effort, and creative implementation of your service or product will help you increase your competence as an entrepreneur.

⊛ **Exclude outsiders.** Heed your own inner voice and learn from your own past experiences and those of your mentors how to forge your own path in entrepreneurship. Ignore the naysayers, the meddlers, the critics, and the pessimists, all of whom can pollute your theory of mind, about yourself and others around you. I recommend these two books for more insight into this principle:

- Bramson, Robert (1981). *Coping With Difficult People.* New York: Dell Publishing.

- Glass, Lillian (1995). *Toxic People.* New York: St. Martin's Griffin.

Timing

HOW OFTEN have you heard the phrase, "Timing is everything"? As a pediatric speech therapist specializing in treating young children with autism, I've lived this phrase for years while trying to facilitate my students' underdeveloped theory of mind and sensory processing skills, both of which contributed to my students' disorientation regarding person, place, and time. This resulted in behavioral and social communication challenges because of a mind-body disconnect between executive functioning on the one hand and episodic memory and the neurological monitoring of time (your internal body clock) on the other.

Think about what it feels like to be jet-lagged. Think about the last time you were in a different time zone and your sleep cycle changed, or you found yourself starving at odd hours of the night. How should you work on the metacognitive skill of time management? By honing your ability to truly live in the moment while simultaneously adapting to changes in routine for that moment in time. That means accomplishing tasks in segments, being resilient when obstacles arise, and fine-tuning or altering your plans as needed to complete your objectives.

Time management is thus a sentient behavior like any other, like economics. Economics, as the Freakonomics Duo (Steven Levitt and Stephen Dubner) repeatedly demonstrate, should really be listed as a *behavioral science* course in college curricula, not a business course. If it were maybe I would have taken it, and more women in education and healthcare (two historically female-saturated industries) would have been eager to take the course.

Timing is the driving force behind economic expansion and disruptive innovation. Cognitive (behavioral and deliberate) timing. Think of it in terms of character development, the unfolding good vs. evil struggle, and the subsequent behaviors of characters over a season of meticulously planned story arcs portrayed on weekly TV shows. Think of it in terms of the current practice of premiering a movie in select theaters first to generate buzz, and then inviting critics to view the film, write about it, and thus prepare the masses for later viewing.

Timing involves not only committing yourself to seeing a project through but to using your theory of mind to continuously and methodically adapt to your milieu. To alter your own actions, innate or learned, in response to environmental changes, which may be organic or behavioral in nature and which result from changes in the topography and behavior of those in that ecosystem.

Joss Whedon, in his varied works and real-life actions, exemplifies this idea. This idea of cognitive timing that you can hone, based upon your adaptive behaviors and actions. The brilliant mind behind some of the greatest portrayals of female empowerment on television, the expert on slowly unveiling multidimensionalities and adaptive capabilities of good vs. evil, Whedon is a true master of cinematic timing. He has created some of the most innovative, compelling characters, as well as story lines, in Hollywood. I've watched and studied them all. Repeatedly. I say that out loud. I say that with pride. I do get some weird looks. But I've found my own inner landscape psychologically and intellectually enriched by viewing his creations, both as a human being and an entrepreneur.

As seen in his critically acclaimed TV shows *Buffy the Vampire Slayer, Angel, Firefly, Dollhouse,* and his recent movie *The Avengers,* Whedon knows that true villains are more complex than they appear on the surface. He knows that our perspective about them changes with context and their ability to adapt, which causes us to then adapt our thinking about them and their actions accordingly. His richly drawn characters, impeccable timing, and morally ambiguous cautionary tales, repeatedly interwoven into story lines, have spawned an entire movement of academic, religious, and feminist debates about each episode, entire seasons, or connecting story arcs. In fact, there's a huge online community forum (http://bit.ly/discovering-buffy) where real people have come forward from various locations and educational backgrounds, both men and women, explaining how they came to watch *Buffy the Vampire Slayer.* People from various walks of life and viewpoints.

The Whedon-verse is a unique domain where the human observers, especially entrepreneurs, can practice theory of mind (perspective, empathy), outside-the-box thinking, and cognitive-based timing. There we find ourselves appreciating the journey, not just the end result, while engaging in shameless voyeurism of the soul, inexplicably rooting for the bad guys. This is a hallmark reaction to this bard's impeccable timing and execution of events in the Buffy-verse or Angel-verse.

The villains of Whedon's unique universes are all cleverly portrayed with hidden depths, nuanced revelations, and surprising behaviors at unexpected intervals. These portrayals are done with intelligence and underlying compassion. I'm referring to Angel and Spike, who shrewdly demonstrate their deep struggle with their journey, their process of achieving purpose. They constantly struggle with their duality and their sometimes thwarted attempts to subsequently adapt. You see this as well in the ambiguous heroes of *The Avengers*, namely The Black Widow and The Hulk. They are also struggling with their duality and need to adapt.

In a stellar display Joss Whedon and his many well-drawn characters have personified the concept of disruptive innovation (adaptive reboots) through motives, actions, and subsequent reactions to the events surrounding their story. When interviewed in April 2012 by *The New York Times* (http://bit.ly/film-superheroes-include-director) about his perspective on the industry behind blockbuster Hollywood movies (right before *The Avengers* hit the big screen), Whedon joked about his mixed feelings and own actions saying, "That doesn't make me a hypocrite, it just gives me layers."

Like the shifting of the earth's tectonic plates, your layers (theory of mind) can affect your timing and ability to adapt, to alter outcomes and trajectories, overtly or not. As an entrepreneur you need to keep this in mind when thinking about timing, strategy, and the end-game — how to play the ultimate chess game on an ever-changing board.

Interestingly, the term *disruptive innovation* was first used in Clayton Christenson's 1997 book, *The Innovator's Dilemma*, the same year *Buffy the Vampire Slayer* aired. The show lasted for seven seasons. *Angel,* the spin-off series created in 1999, ran for five seasons.

Patterns. More seemingly random events but actually parts of a pattern to ponder. There's a sense of timing in everything — nature, personal growth, and entrepreneurship. Below are suggestions to follow to become a more competent entrepreneur, in sync with your environment and those in it. These suggestions will enable you to be ready to implement disruptive innovation to effect change, especially in the fields of education and healthcare (where female employees have historically resided and are thus poised to be pioneers).

Penina's Pointers

How to Build Entrepreneurial Competency

1. **Be educated.** Learn and achieve in your chosen field. Specialize in your chosen field, and practice in that field for as long as it takes to establish proficiency and familiarity with best practices. Start small and find opportunities to slowly branch out. Tie your knowledge to your business practices. Learn new things and new business practices — online, in workshops, in books. Share what you've learned with others. Work to gain your credentials and street cred over time via networking, physically and digitally. Find a mentor, maybe a few.

2. **Be heard.** Establish your service or product and target your niche market. Write trade articles and thought-provoking comments for other people's writings

online, choosing wisely where to let your voice be heard. When giving presentations and sales pitches remember: Use the positive language of emotional attunement, change, and humor to further your brand.

3. **Be seen.** Build a figurative topiary — a visually appealing execution of your business plan — and nurture it.

   ❀ Communicate with prospective clients and seasoned ones who already know you.

   ❀ Organize your internal and external paper trail for better time management.

   ❀ Use technology and social media to create a visible digital footprint for your company.

   ❀ Choose to accept or decline venture capital and handle your bootstrapping adventures well — financially, mentally, and ethically.

4. **Be respected.** Remember the theory of multiple intelligences and how your strengths are your assets. How honing your perspective can help you transition from a *me* to a *we* mentality as needed. Be perceived as being empathic, a good reader of people, adaptable, timely, and multidimensional. Protect your physical and digital reputation.

5. **Be bold.** Keep up with the latest trends in your industry and in the technology arena. Look for patterns to help you have that eureka moment showing you how you can promote change. Creatively and systematically look to fill in a gap in the proverbial supply and demand seesaw that fuels any economy and global market. There has never been a better time to join the Entrepreneurial Revolution as a leader, not just a follower.

The Power of a Mentor:
Where to Find One, How to Keep One,
and When to Discard One

KEY WEBSITES

- http://bit.ly/why-female-entrepreneurs-need-mentors
- http://bit.ly/why-smart-bosses-treat-employees-like-dogs
- http://bit.ly/mentors-versus-advisors
- http://bit.ly/5-things-seasoned-entrepreneurs-know
- http://bit.ly/work-challenges-facing-women-as-they-age
- http://bit.ly/finding-great-startup-mentors
- http://bit.ly/9-rules-for-stifling-innovation
- http://bit.ly/go-from-employee-to-entrepreneur
- http://bit.ly/mentorship-past-present-future
- http://bit.ly/benefits-of-mentoring
- http://bit.ly/mentoring-manual
- http://bit.ly/sponsorship-vs-mentorship
- http://bit.ly/engaging-mentors
- http://bit.ly/reverse-mentoring-for-young-leaders
- http://bit.ly/forget-mentors
- http://bit.ly/success-for-entrepreneurial-women

Quotes to Ponder

*You grow up the day you have the first real laugh — at
yourself.*

— Ethel Barrymore

*The more we are aware of our basic paradigms, maps,
or assumptions, and the extent to which we have been
influenced by our experience, the more we can … listen to
others and be open to their perceptions, thereby getting a
larger picture and a far more objective view.*

— Stephen Covey

Definition

Mentor: One who gives advice and instruction regarding the course
or process to be followed.

— *The Merriam-Webster Dictionary*

THE PROTOTYPE for today's mentor is attributed to Homer's *The
Odyssey*. Homer introduces the reader to Mentor, the best friend
who protects and raises Odysseus's son, Telemachaus, while his father is away. Mentorship as a process was later attributed to Florence
Nightingale, who is credited with having founded the nursing profession as we know it. The term was used during the feminist movement of the 1960s. It was used again in the 1980s and 90s to refer to
a practice seen in North American businesses.

The concept of internship, a rite of passage in so many professional fields today, has its roots in mentorship, although the dynamics and paradigms vary from industry to industry. I experienced
both internship and mentorship while getting my undergraduate
and graduate degrees in speech-language pathology. Both are built

into the process of acquiring this particular degree in the form of specific, timed, and documented observation and practicum hours (pro bono service) and course requirements.

It's still standard practice today in the field of speech-language pathology (and in many other professions as well) to hire someone whose sole job description involves supervising and mentoring students and other speech therapists. The purpose of this practice is to have an organic system for evaluating performance, supporting education of best practices, and providing professional tweaking by giving constructive criticism (in a humorous, noninsulting, way) and opportunities to emulate a role model.

Across all professions, those who have gained experience and set standards to which others should aspire are usually the ones who end up being mentors. I say usually because, as many people know, mentorship can be a rocky, frustrating experience that doesn't always live up to the hype. In my two decades of practice as both a speech therapist and educational technology consultant, I've been given mentors or have come across possible mentors who in the end were not a good fit for me psychologically, economically, or geographically.

I've been a mentor on best practices in speech therapy, special education, behavior management in autism, social skills development, and technology. I've gone to many conferences as a mentee. I've trained many school-based professionals in various aspects of educational technology over the past 20 years. I've had the pleasure and privilege of being a clinical supervisor of undergraduate and graduate students seeking a degree in speech-language pathology. I have thus been both a mentor and mentee and have learned the value of sitting on both sides of the table. I have gained the knowledge and resources to help me put the puzzle pieces together and network for myself, my clients, and my profession. The gatekeeper of my profession, the American Speech-Language Hearing Association (the speech therapist's version of a union), has devised an entire mentoring protocol that can be downloaded as a PDF (http://bit.ly/mentoring-manual).

Self-education and educating others are predicated on the idea of scaffolding previously learned skills and applying them to new situations or events you've experienced. To that end it's no surprise that entrepreneurship, known for its atmosphere of fast-paced, carpe-diem unpredictability, has made mentorship increasingly pivotal and sought after. Mentors are much-coveted and valuable assets for entrepreneurs because:

- ✿ Their experiences help entrepreneurs, especially newly minted ones, make sense of and navigate often unchartered territory, on many levels.

- ✿ Their contacts help entrepreneurs expand their own network — a real coup in today's ever-expanding virtual address book (because of social media).

- ✿ Their advice can highlight avenues to leadership by pinpointing entrepreneurs' strengths and weaknesses, leading to purposeful searches for other mentors to augment skill sets, strategize how to bridge gaps, and provide support — emotional, financial, and cognitive.

The last is a key benefit of mentorship that needs to be addressed in the world of commerce. In January 2013 John Kotter wrote an article for *Forbes* magazine entitled, "The Often Overlooked but Invaluable Benefits of Mentorship" (http://bit.ly/overlooked-benefits-of-mentorship). In it he writes about the often overlooked benefit of mentorship: facilitation of the development of leadership. "We learn a great deal about management principles and practices in school.," says Kotter. "Leadership, though more popularly discussed in school now, is still more often learned outside of school. The value of a mentor who can help cultivate leadership skills one-on-one, in real-time, reduce the anxiety in taking big steps, and focus leaders on achieving their goals is huge."

In February 2013 *The Huffington Post* published an article by Sejal Hathi, a Yale University student, entitled, "Why Young Female Entrepreneurs Need Mentors" (http://bit.ly/why-female-entrepreneurs-need-mentors). Hathi is the ambassador to Loreal USA's For Girls in Science initiative, which is an entrepreneurial platform for girls to find role models, resources, and support for studying and entering the arenas of STEM (science, technology, engineering, and math). Hathi writes, "We believe that all girls are a powerful movement: a brilliant and unstoppable force that can solve even the world's most intractable challenges, if only they are granted the tools and opportunity. As a young woman social entrepreneur, this worries me. It worries me because I see thousands of girls fearing to engage creatively with technology, and technology is the language of social innovation. The reasons for this situation are crisply clear: Today's innovators in the realms of technology, business, science, enterprise — in the public as well as the private sector — are overwhelmingly men."

This is true, but it doesn't mean that these men don't make good role models or mentors. It just means that some mentors, due to different biological hard-wiring (resulting in a different theory of mind and emotional attunement) and technical proficiency (due to experience, not necessarily aptitude or intelligence), are more suited for specific areas of teaching to help you, the female entrepreneur, attain your goals and leadership skills and up your tech-savvy quotient.

At the same time, it's empowering and inspiring for female entrepreneurs to find female mentors, especially ones who have made it and are willing to generously share their time and knowledge to further the collective aspirations and accomplishments of their gender. In my opinion, it's both a privilege and an imperative for female entrepreneurs to engage in mentorship, whether in real time or online via virtual mentorship forums (thought leadership blogs, social media). There's an element of social entrepreneurship involved that begins when women empower and help other women. There are four women who are on my radar for having done this, and done this well. I recommend that you glean lessons by taking advantage of the free, accessible, and trailblazing virtual mentorship being offered by:

- ❀ Rieva Lesonsky, CEO, GrowBiz Media, and an expert on female entrepreneurship (http://bit.ly/rieva-lesonsky-articles)

- ❀ Geri Stengel, President, The Ventureneer, and an expert on social entrepreneurship (http://bit.ly/geri-stengel)

- ❀ Colleen DenBaise, Director of Digital Media, The Story Exchange, and an expert on digital entrepreneurship (http://thestoryexchange.org)

- ❀ Diane Bertolin, Founder, The Collective Publishing Company, and an expert on social media and author of the archetypal consulting blog series (http://www.thecollectivepc.com)

I'm interested in the concept of mentorship, especially as it relates to female entrepreneurs, because I've learned the importance of collaboration and guidance in my two decades working as a school-based speech therapist. I've lived it as a professional keynote speaker and iPad evangelist on the road throughout North America. I've seen it in our fast-paced, tech-driven, increasingly competitive work environments and startup culture. There's a pressing need for both mentorship and sponsorship of female entrepreneurs, especially in corporate America. We have somehow allowed *The Hunger Games* paradigm to take hold in our minds, to affect our own theory of mind and our willingness to empower other women to "break the glass ceiling" and match skills and wits with their male counterparts, or worse, their female "mirrors."

On 22 May 2013, I read an eloquent, profoundly moving article by Rieva Lesonsky, CEO of GrowBiz Media. It gave background and voice to the rumored dark side of success for women in the workplace years ago. She shared her own experiences and recalled how in the past, "women had to fight against...the belief that women were women's worst enemies — that successful women didn't want other women to succeed." It was known as the Queen Bee syndrome. Lesson learned: Queen Bees are evil. We women have a duty and obligation to be there for one another. As Madeleine Albright, the first female Secretary of State once said, "There is a special place in Hell for women who don't help other women."

It's no surprise that Rieva has become a sought-after, well-respected thought leader and prolific writer about female empowerment and entrepreneurship and one of my favorite virtual mentors. I contacted her directly after reading this article (http://bit.ly/success-for-entrepreneurial-women), which changed my entrepreneurial trajectory and thus my life.

On 11 July 2013 in Ashley Milne-Tyte's blog, *The Broad Experience: A Conversation About Women, The Workplace, and Success,* Anne Libby wrote a thought-provoking post that caught my attention (http://bit.ly/sponsorship-vs-mentorship). The post appeared to be advocating for female entrepreneurs to spend time and energy on pursuing a sponsor instead of a mentor. To quote the blogpost, which quotes Sylvia Ann Hewlitt, author of *Forget a Mentor, Find a Sponsor,* "Women seem to see work relationships as friendships, not something to be used for advancement." It seems to indicate that for female entrepreneurs, in particular, trying to succeed means trying to get sponsorship — from a man!

I disagree with both implications: that sponsors are better than mentors and that women don't think about using their work relationships with other women to get ahead. I do agree with the supposition that, in many cases, men are often sponsors by default, because of their career placement and trajectory and their wider experiences with tech.

On 25 September 2013 I had the pleasure and honor of attending the first female entrepreneurship conference for women startup founders in New York City. I saw examples of both sponsorship and mentorship first-hand over the course of the day, and even got to meet Colleen DeBaise and Geri Stengel in person, which was quite exciting. They are two of my favorite virtual mentors whose writings have profoundly impacted me and my mission. I must say that I'm both a frequent conference attendee and presenter, and I've almost "seen it all." But I was impressed with the WomanCon 2013 program. It was organized by Laura Leites and Adrienne Garland, who hit every note like the meticulous, timely conductors they are. Not every conference is orchestrated like a well-oiled machine. This one was a symphony of scheduled talks and interwoven, structured networking opportunities over a six-hour period, to meet and greet and find women willing to talk to you, help you, and even stay in touch and mentor you down the road.

So what are you, as someone who may be a woman interested in the pursuit of entrepreneurship, to do right now? I would say that it makes sense for to pursue a mentor first (in real time and online) and a sponsor second. Why? Because the real disruptors of innovation come from unexpected places (http://bit.ly/disrupting-disruptive innovation). So you should:

1. Find a mentor, maybe several, to help you get started on the process of becoming an entrepreneur, especially given today's multitasking, *Hunger Game* paradigms so often seen in startup cultures around the world, but especially in the United States.

2. Engage the interest of a sponsor, even a male one, by bartering: *Use reverse mentorship as leverage.* What does that mean? I'll explain soon.

3. Make sure to keep the roles and relationships straight — different folks, different focus. Also, never treat either like a minion, and, no, that's not what interns are for.

But I must warn you — gender loyalty is a myth. I've spent years in a workplace that's largely female because of the nature and financial realities of special education, speech therapy in particular. I've learned the hard way that female-female mentorship, while sometimes more intuitive, can be as political, fraught with competition (if not more), and as ineffective as male-female mentorship. I think that these problems are due to the necessities of job multitasking and company downsizing as well as the inherent fear of change and the difficulty in learning new technology often displayed by old-school female employers and employees in leadership positions today. I've seen this behavior repeatedly among female leaders and female mentors.

Think about the movie *Working Girl,* which showcases the politics seen in female-dominated business settings. Think about Tess, the mentee, a street-smart, minimally educated but very intelligent, hardworking woman, played by Melanie Griffith (one of her best roles). With integrity she creatively finds patterns, based on newspaper articles, to exploit for commercial gain — that is, to get promoted from her position in the typing pool. Tess shows up her corrupt boss and self-appointed mentor, Katherine, an educated but emotionally and morally stunted female executive, played by a competent and viciously funny Sigourney Weaver.

That 1980s movie, which offers a terrific bird's eye view into workforce dynamics of that era, still resonates with me and with many other female employees. If I had to give an example of the worst mentors, however, I would have to go with Katherine or Miranda from *The Devil Wears Prada,* both of whom you really want to yell at, or worse. My friends and I still yell at the screen whenever we get together and watch both vixens in action. So what does a good mentor act like, and how will you know whether a mentor is worth keeping?

Penina's Pointers

Ten Qualities to Look for in a Mentor
(listed in descending level of importance)

1. Accessible: physically and emotionally

2. Diverse background and thinking (to help you see other viewpoints)

3. Solution-oriented; offers constructive criticism

4. Detail-oriented approach to mentoring (follows the script and provides guidance for both the basics and the minutiae of the process)

5. Well-connected and well-respected in chosen field

6. Able to improvise

7. Sense of humor

8. Asks questions about your service or product, philosophy, and timeline

9. Collaborative: admits mistakes and shares the glory

10. Technologically aware (doesn't need to be savvy, but needs to be aware and somewhat knowledgeable in order to share common language or common ground with you)

How to Keep a Mentor

Penina's Five-Step Problem-Solving Hierarchy and Implications for Entrepreneurs

In 2010 I copyrighted and trademarked my preschool social skills curriculum, for children with autism/special needs, entitled, "Socially Speaking™ for Young Children with Autism/

Special Needs: A Practical Social Skills Resource." In it, and in a 2011 subsequent article I wrote for the speech therapy magazine *Advance,* I show how problem solving, an area particularly challenging for youngsters with autism spectrum disorders, is the pinnacle skill seen in people with social communication proficiency (http://bit.ly/social-skills-in-young-children).

Social communication proficiency is needed for both effective mentorship and entrepreneurship. It's especially needed to successfully transition your thinking from *me* to *we* as needed — at home, at work, in life, and in your own perceptions about your reality.

It's crucial that a mentor and entrepreneur understand both the language and the process of problem solving. To quote myself, "Differences in theory of mind in children with ASD can account for difficulty recognizing, interpreting, and resolving problems that are of a social nature. I consider problem solving to be the cornerstone and most advanced skill of good social skill development." My Socially Speaking™ problem-solving hierarchy involves five steps:

1. An awareness that a problem exists, why it exists, and how to react

2. Verbalizing the problem to explain what it is and why it's occurring

3. Exploring solutions, outcomes, and options verbally and calmly

4. Using verbal negotiation to come to an agreement or compromise

5. Resolving conflict, accepting outcomes, and repairing communication breakdowns

Entrepreneurship requires the ability to adapt to your circumstances while simultaneously finding new ways to positively exploit them and implement change. It stands to reason then that a mentor must exhibit characteristics and execute behaviors that are in sync with those of the entrepreneurial mentee, namely verbal and philosophical improvisation for further innovation. Only then can the entrepreneur truly benefit from the mentor's outlook, perspective, and advice. A mentor who displays these traits as well as effective problem solving, in both discussion and execution, is certainly worth holding on to.

Chunking vs. Multitasking
Written agendas and structured interruptions vs. scaffolding and readiness indicators

Over the meandering course of my career as a speech therapist, where I was both a mentor and mentee, I've learned the value of discovering and using patterns — in the way I see the world, treat my clients and students, and approach the process of mentorship. To me, successful mentorship is all about connecting the dots to build a framework for appropriate conduct and best practices, no matter which industry you're in. To that end, I've divided up my modus operandi into *chunking* vs. *multitasking*. Chunking is where I write down all possible agendas — the big picture: what I want to accomplish, how I plan to do so, and which outcomes I anticipate. I then leave a digital trail, often via e-mail, usually entitled "Future Topics to Address" or "Questions to Answer," where instead of getting sidetracked during my allotted meeting time, or interrupting the workflow (of the mentor or the mentee) when I have an epiphany, I leave a breadcrumb trail in advance that can be referred to later and at regular intervals.

Successful mentorship is also about top-down learning, which involves multitasking — breaking down ideas and lessons into two categories: scaffolding and readiness indicators. Multitasking in both mentorship and entrepreneurship involves a methodical breakdown of the steps and areas of learning and then creatively and holistically reconfiguring a desired outcome in a more innovative manner.

That means that I use my knowledge of part-whole relationships to scaffold (layer) my approach to creating disruptive innovation. I also apply this to the practice of problem solving. In addition I've learned to pay careful attention to patterns of behavior, namely readiness indicators, to signal that it's time for me to implement the next step of my business plan.

A practical example of this can be found in the timeline of my own journey as an entrepreneur. In 2009 I began informally lecturing to professionals in my field about my innovative Socially Speaking™ Social Skills Curriculum. I was fully aware that I was offering a product to a niche market, with limited funds for marketing, in the midst of an awful recession. Nonetheless, I copyrighted and trademarked my manuscript and tried to publish it, but the Great Recession caused many interested publishers to put me on hold. I didn't let that stop me. In 2010 I started my own company, Socially Speaking™ LLC, and made use of various free, online social media to spread word about my mission, provide inbound content marketing, and create a forum where

I could create, nurture, and expand my tribe. It was (and still is) a work in progress, which I then expanded by creating my series of Socially Speaking™ Seminars. I began to present them throughout North America in 2011. In 2012 I launched my own version of disruptive innovation, namely my social skills assessment protocol, the Socially Speaking™ iPad App. In my field there are very few digitized evaluations, let alone social skills development assessments. There are also many technophobes in the world of special education — because of lack of funds and lack of experience — interacting with technology. I think this will change. It has to change. So while some have told me I jumped the gun, I'm sticking to my business plan. And still analyzing patterns. And adapting. To orchestrate change.

In special education, the term *readiness indicator* is used in reference to prerequisite skills (behaviors) that need to be altered and/or displayed before clinical implementation of a goal (to foster a skill in the next stage of development). This principle can be applied to entrepreneurial mentorship as well. A good mentor provides the mentee with both knowledge and self-awareness of the necessary prerequisite skills and foundations to build in order to foster change.

Balancing Mentorship and Reverse Mentorship

Jack Welch, former CEO of electronics behemoth GE (General Electric Company), coined the term reverse mentorship during an in-house initiative. Five hundred top GE executives were paired with younger employees for a set amount of time. The goal was for the younger employees to teach the older ones about technology and how to use the Internet (http://bit.ly/reverse-mentoring). Besides increasing the execs' tech IQ this program helped many of the old-school thinkers become better mentors. The morale of many of the young employees was boosted by these empowering opportunities. In addition these young employees had the chance to apply practical leadership strategies early in their careers. Since you've read this far you know the importance of varied experiences for building episodic memory to facilitate your theory of mind.

Effective mentorship is both psycho-social and intellectual in that both the mentor and mentee need to feel that the process is a two-way street. Historically mentorship has been a symbiotic relationship where both parties benefited emotionally and socially from their mutual association. That's why thought leadership is one of the most pivotal uses of social media today. Virtual mentorship, a term I've coined, is the result of careful content curation online. One that fuels the giver's emotional satisfaction in providing teachable moments for others en mass. One that also increases the taker's intellect and grasp of buzzwords, concepts, and trends that are culturally and economically relevant, thus giving him or her social relevance as well.

Today's paradigm shift in commerce, technological innovation, and education requires a radical change in thinking about mentorship and in how to do it effectively. That's why reverse mentorship and those who engage in it are to be commended and emulated. Successful mentorship must now include bartering and payment of currency — the facilitation of commercial, technological, cultural, and social relevance — for it to be lucrative, financially and cognitively.

Helping others feel competent provides a sense of belonging and wellbeing, a feeling of fitting in and not being anachronistic. This is what reverse mentorship is all about. Life today demands a delicate balance between teaching and learning all day long, no matter what your vocation. For more information, I recommend Joel Garfinkle's article from January 2013 on reverse mentorship's three requirements to transform leadership dynamics and organizational paradigms and their benefits (http://bit.ly/reverse-mentoring-for-young-leaders).

There's a growing need for reverse mentorship—for newly initiated entrepreneurs and employees in today's workforce to hone their teaching and mentoring skills early on so that they can accrue experiences that result in the growth of their leadership skills. These young entrepreneurs and employees are also needed to facilitate the cognizance and longevity of seasoned, talented, dedicated, and capable older employees—people who need not retire early, on the dot at 65, or become part-time workers like the preceding generations. Because they live longer lives, have better overall healthcare, and have increased opportunities for education, entrepreneurs and employees, let alone mentors and mentees, have the means to keep learning. To keep growing intellectually and thereby expanding their professional capacity and to promote change. Continual learning is especially relevant for female entrepreneurs.

In May 2012, in honor of Mother's Day, an organization called OWL published a disturbing report entitled, "Women and the Workforce: Challenges and Opportunities Facing Women as They Age" (http://bit.ly/work-challenges-facing-women-as-they-age). The article, written by and referring to a consortium of viewpoints, attempts to inform and strategize about the plight of "older women workers ... facing an array of obstacles in the workplace. Through this report, we endeavor to highlight the critical role these women play in our nation's economy, the special problems they face, and the opportunities all of us can pursue to maximize their full potential."

The article is important to read for many reasons, but especially because of the chart "Application of nine types of leadership behaviors by women and men." This chart, adapted from a 2008 study by McKinsey & Company, "Women Matter 2," lists nine desirable leadership behaviors that are applied by both women and men. I invite you to test yourself and others with this list. Which of the following leadership behaviors do you apply?

1. People development

2. Expectations and rewards

3. Role model

4. Inspiration

5. Participative decision making

6. Intellectual stimulation

7. Efficient communication

8. Individualistic decision making

9. Control and corrective action

I would argue that these leadership behaviors can be fostered in an entrepreneurial atmosphere where reverse mentorship is practiced. These behaviors are deliberate actions that are ingrained, not just through experience but through education, innovation, and problem solving. An entrepreneurial mentor, no matter gender or age, who can adjust his or her thinking to accommodate the behaviors of the mentee based upon the mentee's differing theory of mind and episodic memory is worth keeping. Certainly worth holding onto for a long time.

When to Discard a Mentor

Discard a mentor when the following behavioral traits, listed in descending levels of importance, are repeatedly displayed:

1. Poor problem-solving skills

2. Poor time-management and organizational skills

3. Insincerity

4. Lack of risk aversion

5. Lack of curiosity

6. Communication breakdowns

7. Overconfidence

8. Inflexiblility

9. Disinterest in your actual service or product even though there may be interest in your accomplishments as a person or professional (translation: wants a free ride)

10. Technophobia (this will interfere with your own time-management, organizational, and communication skills with said mentor)

The Pitfalls of Perfectionism

KEY WEBSITES

- ⌐ http://bit.ly/pitfalls-of-perfectionism
- ⌐ http://bit.ly/perfectionism-is-the-enemy
- ⌐ http://bit.ly/is-being-a-perfectionist-hurting-business
- ⌐ http://bit.ly/inside-the-minds-of-perfectionists
- ⌐ http://bit.ly/blast-past-perfectionism
- ⌐ http://bit.ly/why-perfectionism-kills-creativity
- ⌐ http://bit.ly/things-i-learned-trying-to-have-it-all

Quotes to Ponder

Perfection is not a quest for the best. It is a pursuit of the worst in ourselves, the part that tells us that nothing we do will ever be good enough — that we should try again.

— Julia Cameron

The closest to perfection a person ever comes is when he fills out a job application form.

— Stanley Randall

Definition

Perfectionism: A disposition to regard anything short of perfection as unacceptable.

— *The Merriam-Webster Dictionary*

THE PSYCHOLOGICAL STUDY of perfectionism and the subsequent literature, an offshoot of the public phenomenon of introspection (which gained momentum in the 1980s), suggests that this behavioral trait is perceived as a figurative Olympic medal. A medal proudly worn by über-efficient and competent people who view it as the price to be paid for providing top-tier performances in a chosen field. Dr. David Burns sheds light on the inner dialogue of a perfectionist in his 1980 article for *Psychology Today*, "The Perfectionist's Script for Self Defeat" (http://bit.ly/perfectionist-script-for-self-defeat). He writes, "Driven to create a flawless product, perfectionists can't sense when the point of diminishing returns has been reached."

I believe that perfectionism is a dangerous trait for entrepreneurs to have and one that, paradoxically, seems to thrive in the workplace. I've actually seen other entrepreneurs at conferences and trade shows attempt to hone and proudly show off their perfectionist tendencies. Tendencies that are not in keeping with the strong evidence about what it takes to succeed. It certainly isn't in keeping with the messages I am trying to convey in this book.

Dr. Burns, a psychiatrist and a mentor (an assistant professor), seems quite concerned about "self-defeating perfectionist attitudes" to the point that he actually devised a self-evaluation checklist, The Perfectionism Scale, found in his article. In it he gives the reader phraseology to think about regarding setting standards, making mistakes, and future expectations that provide insight into their resiliency quotient and their emotional IQ.

Earlier in this book I attempted to show correlations between emotional attunement and resiliency. Resiliency, which is essentially the neuro-cognitive coping mechanism that's triggered when you face changes or obstacles, is a behavioral trait that's both innate and learned. It stems from:

⊛ The emotional ability to self-regulate (manage stress) through humor and optimism by accessing your theory of mind (perspective)

⊛ The intellectual ability to access episodic memory to foster problem solving (improvisation or adaptability)

Dr. Burns's sentiments echo mine when he points out that "perfectionists also see themselves as inefficient because they tend to imagine that successful people achieve personal goals with minimal effort, few errors, maximal self-confidence, and little, if any, emotional distress. Because of this fantasy, perfectionists are likely to view their own quite human coping efforts as inadequate."

Much research has since been done on the topics of over-confidence, perfectionism, and obsessive-compulsive disorder (OCD). A lot of the recent studies on these subjects are being funded on behalf of children with autism. There is a premise, which may or may not be correct, that these traits, which result in rigid behavior and thinking, are quite prevalent in this population. They therefore require study and treatment because they are quite destructive — socially, cognitively, and academically. An overview of this particular research is beyond the scope of this book. But it seems that there's another demographic that should be considered for future research: entrepreneurs! I hope doctoral students are taking note.

Perfectionism is unhealthy for entrepreneurs to inculcate and aspire to for three reasons:

1. It creates a dichotomy between belief and behavior by fostering negative us-vs.-them thinking, which I believe deters the entrepreneur's positive intent to transition from a *me*- to a *we*-style performance to effect change.

2. It creates a false reality of how things actually are vs. how they should be, leading to skewed perceptions and stagnant innovation.

3. It creates either heightened inner anxiety and/or arrogance, resulting in disconnected emotional attunement with others and leading to an underdeveloped or fragmented theory of mind (perspective, empathy), which prevents entrepreneurs from attempting to deliver their hook, rally their tribe, and accept and/or provide mentorship.

Today's startup culture is fiercely competitive — a show of both financial and psychological warfare. Added to the mix is the increasing need for technologically savvy, multidirectional marketing, and the use of social media. Playing the game, let alone entering the arena of entrepreneurship, requires agile, habituated, and reactive mental gymnastics to quickly sort through seemingly random patterns to find commonalities. To take those sometimes unremarkable patterns, those low-key findings, and transform them into decisive, creative, "bling-y" actions. Actions that are publicized in splashy, attention-getting ways on social media sites.

Successful entrepreneurship thus requires constant vigilance and perseverance. You need to cope with the constant stream of information and ever-changing technology. An unfortunate side effect of all this seems to be a rise in perfectionism.

In May 2013 Amanda Neville wrote an incisive article for *Forbes* magazine entitled, "Perfectionism is the Enemy of Everything" (http://bit.ly/perfectionism-is-the-enemy). In it she lists three types of perfectionism and how they can be toxic to entrepreneurs:

1. Self-oriented perfectionism, in which individuals impose high standards on themselves

2. Socially prescribed perfectionism, where individuals feel that others expect them to be perfect

3. Other-oriented perfectionism, in which individuals place high standards on others

In this thought-provoking, shrewd article, Neville raises some interesting questions about the effect of perfectionism on having perspective and on mentorship. These are two behaviors seen in entrepreneurial circles that result from the need for flexible improvisation, especially in the educational technology and healthcare industries. Neville suggests that the entrepreneurial need to heed criticism as a mentee, and later give it as a mentor, is impeded by perfectionism because it quashes the desires to ask for help, see others' viewpoints and empathize, and promote teamwork. The article even provides a link for the reader to take a perfectionism quiz: http://bit.ly/perfectionism-quiz.

How do you counteract perfectionism? Perhaps by being more introspective and retraining your responses and behavior? That's what Esther Crain seems to be suggesting in her 19 August 2013, article entitled "Five Ways to Blast Perfectionism and Get Your Work Done" (http://bit.ly/blast-past-perfectionism). She advises you to "dial back your perfectionism so you can succeed" by changing the way you think (understand the cause, accept constructive criticism) and the way you act and speak (ask for help, set and prioritize goals).

Psychologists would nod and offer similar strategies, under the umbrella of cognitive behavioral therapy (CBT), to try. As someone who has successfully used elements of CBT in the treatment of children with autism and their sometimes overwhelming, rigid need for sameness and symmetry, I agree that there are ways to reshape behavior — even perfectionism. But as an educator turned entrepreneur, I have to say that in addition to psychology, the Entrepreneurial Revolution itself has given us the antidotes, the means to fight our perfectionist tendencies. Traits that may lie dormant for years until an environmental trigger sets them free. It's the nature vs. nurture debate all over again, only on a different playing field.

What are the antidotes? Adaptability. Resiliency. Optimism. Creativity. Humor.

Adaptability. Resiliency. Also known as *the pivot,* an entrepreneurial tendency to "try out new ideas, shed them quickly if they don't catch on, and move on to the next new thing." This definition was given by writers Lizette Chapman and Emily Maltby in an article published in the *Wall Street Journal*'s small business section in April 2012 entitled, "Pivoting Pays Off for Tech Entrepreneurs" (http://bit. ly/pivoting-pays-for-tech-entrepreneurs). In it they quote venture capitalist Tony Conrad, who says that pivoting "represents some of the best methodology that the Valley has invented. Starting something, determining it's not working, and then leveraging aspects of [that] technology is extremely powerful."

The article ends with an observation of entrepreneurial startup mojo. "Even after what seems like a failure, an ability to quickly adapt is considered a key skill among founders." Adaptability. Resiliency. Optimism. Creativity. Lauded skills that an entrepreneur needs to have to make it. To counteract perfectionism. To effect change.

What is the secret sauce to stir into the pot with all of these other ingredients?

As someone who specializes in social communication skills development in children with autism, where deviations from the script can result in total behavioral melt-downs that cause lost time for everyone involved, not just a loss of revenue or momentum, I would have to say that humor (a byproduct of cognition, executive functioning, and subsequent self-regulation) would be that secret sauce. Humor enables you to take constructive criticism, engage in flexible thinking, and practice stress management.

Let me end this section on building a better entrepreneur with a double-hitter — about perfectionism and its antidote, humor. In 1981 Shel Silverstein published a zany, clever collection of poems, essays, and rhyming and un-rhyming musings, in one tome, *A*

Light in the Attic. In it he wrote a wise poem that I memorized for a school talent show, and repeatedly shared with others for years as both a colleague and mentor. I invite you to read the full poem as well as his other wonderful works. Silverstein truthfully and eloquently captures the spirit and feelings of childhood; his writings still resonate with me today. Here are some partially quoted verses from his poem, "Almost Perfect":

"Almost perfect … but not quite."
Those were the words of Mary Hume
At her seventh birthday party,
Looking 'round the ribboned room
"This tablecloth is pink not white —
Almost perfect … but not quite."

Ninety-eight the day she died
Complainin' 'bout the spotless floor.
People shook their heads and sighed,
"Guess that she'll like heaven more."
Up went her soul on feathered wings,
Out the door, up out of sight.
Another voice from heaven came —
"Almost perfect … but not quite."

FIVE

Final Words on the NICE Philosophy

KEY WEBSITES

- 🖱 http://bit.ly/your-next-hire
- 🖱 http://www.wikipedia.org
- 🖱 http://www.freakonomics.com
- 🖱 https://www.coursera.org
- 🖱 http://sethgodin.typepad.com
- 🖱 http://www.guykawasaki.com
- 🖱 http://bit.ly/women-in-STEM
- 🖱 http://leanin.org
- 🖱 http://bit.ly/mind-technology
- 🖱 http://bit.ly/entrepreneurs-should-be-community-leaders
- 🖱 http://bit.ly/characteristics-entrepreneurs-possess
- 🖱 http://bit.ly/maslow-hierarchy-of-needs
- 🖱 http://bit.ly/bard-internet-revolution-is-sociology
- 🖱 http://bit.ly/solis-overcoming-the-tech-trap
- 🖱 http://bit.ly/solis-change-happens
- 🖱 http://bit.ly/deragon-tech-influence-over-humanity

Quotes to Ponder

*Never believe that a few caring people can't change the world.
For indeed, that's all who ever have.*

— Margaret Mead

*Information is the currency of the Internet. As a medium, the
Internet is brilliantly efficient at shifting information from the
hands of those who have it into the hands of those who do not.*

— Steven Levitt and Stephen Dubner

Definition

Source: A point of origin or procurement, a firsthand document or
primary reference work.

— *The Merriam-Webster Dictionary*

A S A TECH-GEEK WOMAN, and an entrepreneurial woman at that,
I have often felt that I'm a different breed. I certainly feel that
female entrepreneurship is in a class by itself, for better or for worse.
That's why I raised a question for female entrepreneurs, which I hid
in the statement portion of the title of this book: How do you balance your cravings for humanity and technology in today's startup
culture? I also asked another question at the beginning of this book:
Are we women really ready for the Entrepreneurial Revolution and
its sibling, the Tech Revolution?

I want to reiterate that in entrepreneurship the process — the
journey — is *truly* the most important outcome of your venture. You
will learn this as you forge your own paths to achieving your goals, to
implementing your own service or product, and to hopefully be able
to mass produce and effect change. You will see that your landscapes,
your inner one and the outer one around you, will evolve and teach
you new things. Which is good because movement signifies growth.

Movement, migration, transformation, and renewal of the seasons all signify the journey of nature and the built-in potential for change. I believe that change is an inherent right and outcome of being alive, a gift bestowed upon sentient beings by God. It's necessary for your theory of mind, skill set, and legacy, to evolve. The human condition encompasses opportunities and experiences for growth.

Stagnant water breeds disease. The properties and characteristics of water — flowing, nurturing, renewing, and cleansing — are all characteristics for the entrepreneur to reflect on and emulate. *Water* and *information* are two words that evoke a sense of flowing, of movement, of change. The properties of water, including the associated words *source, flow,* and *nourishment,* can all be applied to today's information superhighway, the Internet.

I confess to being a bit of a word lover (I minored in English in college), and my friends know that I've been addicted to the word game Mad Libs for years. In preparation for writing this chapter, I've been pondering the root of the word *source.* Both water and information are viewed as sources that are increasingly valuable commodities in today's global market and to the environmentally conscious gatekeepers of commerce. The one who controls the water's source is the one with the political and economic power. The one who pitches a tent near the flowing water can also benefit greatly and broker power as well.

The same is true of information. Today's thought leaders and social technology/social media experts thrive on the creation of meaningful, marketable content (establishing themselves as voices, sources) and the dissemination of meaningful, marketable content created by others (establishing themselves as resources by directing and repurposing the flow of information). It's therefore crucial for me to treat this chapter as both a source and resource. To provide a summary of all the suggested strategies I've listed in the Penina's Pointers of this book. To provide closing arguments about the validity of my perspective on female entrepreneurship today, viewed through the lens of my NICE approach and philosophy.

If you're like many people and review your game plan, focus on the bottom line, and look at the last chapter of a book before deciding to purchase it (let alone read it), you're in luck. If you're someone who watches a movie trailer before committing to seeing the entire movie, then this next section is for you. In it I'll sum up all of the Penina's Pointers by paring them down to one important quote from *Freakonomics*. A quote that I will interpret for you using my NICE philosophy and using the root word source in three ways:

> *There are three basic flavors of incentive: economic, social, and moral.*
>
> — *Freakonomics*

Penina's Interpretations

How to Think Like an Entrepreneur vs. a Business Owner

Economic Incentives = Think *Open Source.* Be NICE.

I'VE BEEN TOLD that my NICE philosophy has elements of social entrepreneurship in its DNA. I'm not surprised, given my personal and professional background. The Tech Revolution is now also being heralded as the Social Technology Revolution, partly because of the actionable insights and repurposing of thought leadership — distributed content seen on the various social media platforms. But it's also because of the resurgence of interest in the human factor of technology trends, seen in the increasingly collaborative process of enterprise and philanthropic engagement around the world.

The human factor of business and technology trends has been studied since Abraham Maslow introduced the Maslow Hierarchy of

Needs in his 1943 paper, "A Theory of Human Motivation." The paper provided a basic blueprint for people to use to achieve the work/life balance that we all aspire to. It's no surprise that so many industries adopted his paradigm, indoctrinated others in it, and reinterpreted it over time as commerce changed. What does surprise me is that many people minimize the impact of humanity on technology and vice versa. Alexander Bard, Brian Solis, and Jay Deragon have all written and spoken about this phenomenon at length. See the relevant links to read more about their ideas at the start of this chapter.

In his insightful 29 October 2013, blogpost "Being Human Creates Higher Returns" (http://bit.ly/being-human-creates-higher-returns), Jay Deragon writes, "Business leaders are just now recognizing that their business results have a direct correlation to the organization's ability to think, act, speak and feel in human terms. Instead of looking at the enhanced human dynamics created [with social technology], they have merely made it a tool to extend marketing efforts."

Some people don't realize that increased enterprise provides increased opportunities to make life better for others, not just themselves and their inner circle. Not just for those allowed into the inner sanctum of their inner landscape. Economic incentives are meant to motivate you to behave in a specific manner that should (it may not) correlate to a positive outcome. One that can be measured in two ways: time and money. For various reasons these commodities drive entrepreneurship. They are the elusive currencies in today's startup culture. Both are important, but they comprise only a small portion of the big picture — your mission. Business owners spend hours trying to generate income in the short term. Entrepreneurs use time and money to solve problems and create disruptive innovation — for the long term. To effect meaningful, long-lasting, and profound change — in the way people live and interact with their environment and with each other.

Social entrepreneurship, not just time and money, should drive entrepreneurship. Our entrepreneurial practices should add value to the human experience, not detract from it. We need to adopt more of an open source policy in our entrepreneurial best practices. We need more opportunities for social technology to help us think on our own, not just tell us what others are thinking (thought leaders, bloggers) or what we should be thinking (marketers, politicians). It begins with providing more access to open source technology (a development model that provides for free access to and distribution of the product). Why? Open source technology gives us access to information that can be used to connect the dots — about our own lives, our roles, and our realities. So that our inner voice emerges amongst the clamoring of other voices. So that we reflect on and refine our own social and moral consciousness despite the inundating, constant stream of others' consciousnesses.

One great example of open source technology is Pinterest, a digital photo-sharing site considered both Web 2.0 and open source. One of the most popular trends on Pinterest is to post photos (scenic views, graphic designs, etc.) against a visually pleasing backdrop with inspirational and famous quotes by others. As a colleague pointed out to me, "Pinterest is very labor intensive," which is exactly why I think of it as ingenious, disruptive, civic engagement! It takes methodical intent and individuality to assign various quotes to scenic backgrounds, and it takes time and effort to hone your humanity, appreciation for other viewpoints, and awareness of visual aesthetics.

Research has long shown the benefits of dreaming, taking in the scenery, and reading and storytelling. People reap all kinds of benefits, which include emotional well-being, resiliency, creativity, and problem solving ability. These are traits that help us retain our humanity in the face of what can sometimes be a grueling existence. These are traits that help us pursue entrepreneurship in the face of what can sometimes be insurmountable odds. It's hard to be a social entrepreneur, or do any good deed for that matter, when you're struggling to survive, to get some inner peace, to get some sleep.

In her blog, *Brain Pickings,* Maria Popova recently posted a compelling argument: "How Mind Reading and 'Positive Constructive Daydreaming' Enhance Creativity and Improve Our Social Skills" (http://bit.ly/enhancing-creativity). She weaves together interesting perspectives from writer Rebecca McMillan, psychologist Jerome Singer (author of *The Inner World of Day Dreaming*), and psychologist Scott Kaufman (author of *Ungifted: Intelligence Redefined*) to "deliver new insights into how mind-wandering plays an essential, empowering role in daily life and creativity." To quote Singer, "Our human condition is such that we are forever in the situation of deciding how much attention to give to self-generated thought and how much to information from the external social or physical environment."

To me, Singer's quote and the entire blogpost reflect our continuing struggle to positively exploit opportunities in entrepreneurship and to positively harness social technology for the greater good. Just like those Pinterest boards full of quotes. I've used them to raise my spirits and to process and analyze events when I've had a hard day or an argument with someone. I've used them to find quotes to use in my blogposts, at meetings, and during seminars to inspire others. I've used them for researching pithy quotes for this book.

I believe that Pinterest, more than any other social technology platform, encompasses the humanizing and individualization of the give-and-take exchange of social technology. Pinterest's scope and brevity provide succinct calls to action and food for thought that resonate with my own theory of mind, becoming interwoven with my own ideas, plans, and actions. It's more time-consuming physically, but less intrusive mentally. So "pinners" have no choice but to carefully orchestrate their message and curate content that aligns with their mission and brand and their carefully crafted persona, the social technology avatar they present to the world.

Other social technology platforms such as Facebook and Twitter provide more pitfalls for compromising that avatar, by providing an endless stream of ads and personal and professional news of what others are thinking and doing. Google, especially the search engine, used to be better at balancing humanity and technology before it began inundating the viewer with ads and promotions based on their Internet browsing history. I wish Google would instead concentrate on ways to further the education of our fellow human beings by rapidly growing the EdX platform for practical, entrepreneurial, and relevant MOOCs (massive open online courses) and other online courses. I wish it would use open source technology, similar to Wikipedia.

Wikipedia, which was also created to be open source, is another example of being nice about technology use. While not all the information on the site is accurate (readers should be careful), people all over the world have an accessible, free well of information from which to draw. I dare you to say you've never taken advantage of Wikipedia to look something up. Interestingly, it's becoming increasingly popular to contribute information to Wikipedia on a plethora of topics, places, people, and practices. It's becoming a digital storytelling and global "daily journal entry" activity for the masses to engage in, impacting global markets in unforeseen ways.

Wikipedia has already become the living receptacle of data — an ever-evolving, interactive encyclopedia and teaching tool that brings to mind the ancient Library of Alexandria. Intellectual collaboration has been done for centuries, but this cultural phenomenon of technological teamwork is giving our economy a real boost. It's rapidly leveling the playing field for both global students and global entrepreneurs.

Wikipedia recently ran an online campaign to raise funds so that the staff could continue to do what they do. I used PayPal to donate to the cause. I believe in the concept of open source. It's a catalyst for intellectual and emotional growth that results in change. Global change. Economic change. Social change.

Take advantage of the sources of information available to you via open source. What do I recommend?

Technology and the Internet are Your Friends — Treat Them Nicely

Technology (social, mobile, educational, and recreational) and the Internet, when used together in meaningful ways, can collectively help you and others who access it. A friend recently told me about free online courses she was taking using Coursera.org. Another example of open source. My friend was amazed to discover how many people in countries that are technologically less advanced than the United States were taking these courses with her, on diverse subjects such as Art for Beginners and Einstein's Theory of Relativity. Curious, I did a bit of research about Coursera and found an interesting *Inc.* magazine article from 24 June 2013 about it, with entrepreneurial ramifications.

In "Your Next Hire: Foreign, Web Savvy, and Hungry for Challenge" (http://bit.ly/your-next-hire), serial entrepreneur Jeff Hoffman wrote of his experience attending an entrepreneurship summit in Moscow. He describes a new breed of entrepreneur, one who "is not only building a world-class online business, but may show up in your market and compete aggressively."

What's the catalyst? *Educational technology.* Coursera. TED videos. MOOCs. Ease of mobile communications. What's Hoffman's advice for handling these future disruptors and innovators? "Find them. Partner with them. Employ them. This new generation of online-educated entrepreneurs can bring your product or service to their market much faster and more effectively than you can."

Technology is leveling the playing field, especially in entrepreneurial arenas. Hoarding technology is unrealistic and unproductive. It's better to use technology, the Internet, and e-learning opportunities to learn, grow your network, and share those lessons with others. They could be your next business partner, paying customer, or social media follower who raves about you online.

John Jantsch, author of the seminal *Duct Tape Marketing,* hosts "guest-blogger Thursdays" on his blog. A post by Jeff Cobb, author of

Leading the Learning Revolution: The Expert's Guide to Capitalizing on the Exploding Lifelong Education Market, recently caught my eye. In his 1 August 2013, blogpost, "Five Reasons Why Every Business Must Be a Learning Business" (http://bit.ly/be-a-learning-business), Cobb explains why "effective educational content marketing is more important than ever for businesses." One reason that it's important is the customer's need for social interaction about things that matter. It can add value, spark dialogue, build on your existing workflow, and drive sales.

So get started. Learn. Share the wealth. Be nice and give back.

Practice Being Nice

As an entrepreneur implement open source practices with your social media, conduct, and sustainable practices. One of the first things I did when I created my Socially Speaking™ website, at the start of my own entrepreneurial journey (when I knew much less than I know now), was to create a PDF page of information and charts. That anyone can download for free. To keep handy on their screens instead of printing them out. I posted free miscellaneous worksheets and articles from other sources (curated content) in addition to my own. I continue to add to that page every month.

This past year when I gave my Socially Speaking™ iPad Seminars in North America I gave many of my app promo codes to educators to use to help children learn. I even got other iOS app developers to send me a few of their promo codes to donate to my cause. To effect change. Long term. As American journalist Tom Brokaw says, "It's easy to make a buck. It's a lot tougher to make a difference."

I recently came across a website featuring Susan Cain's book, *Quiet,* and her blog, *The Power of Introverts: Join the Quiet Revolution.* While I haven't yet read the book, I was intrigued with her blogposts, which led me to an intriguing post by Charlie Kim, CEO of Next Jump. He recently wrote a beautifully written article about updating Maslow's Hierarchy of Needs for today's business mentality (http://bit.ly/maslow-hierarchy-of-needs). I was impressed with the mantra he attributed to his company's mission: *We use business as a platform to build people of higher character.* At the top of this new Hierarchy of Needs framework is purpose. Kim asks, "Why are we on this planet?" He answers that this question must drive the purpose of any business today. "We have so much to do before leaving this planet … to dramatically change the world in a positive way. One for one isn't good enough, we want to impact millions, maybe even billions."

I couldn't agree more and cannot recommend this viewpoint enough.

Social Incentives = Think *Outsource.* Be INFORMED.

SOCIAL INCENTIVES, such as peer pressure during recess in school, verbal praise, and promotions at work, are all psych-outs that human beings use on themselves and others. As an educator I've seen and used social incentives in a variety of ways, for a variety of reasons: to model good behavior, gain compliance, and motivate others. Social incentives are the opening salvos that educators use with children to foster awareness of proper conduct as a *me* amongst the *we.* To help internalize learned lessons needed to transition from being a *me* to being a *we* in social situations, as needed.

In special education, teachers and therapists teach children with autism, who tend to have socialization challenges, what social incentives are and why they are important to be aware of, even if they're intangible, unlike earlier given reinforcers such as food or toys. It's our job to teach children to learn how to initially anticipate, respond to, and then look forward to social incentives — being singled out for a job well done, being complimented, and being recognized for their performance. This teaching begins with empowering them, planting seeds of self-esteem, and insuring that they know that they are noticed.

All human beings have the innate drive to be noticed. To feel validated and connected, to be seen in a good light, to be viewed as being special and helpful, for putting their best foot forward. It's why verbal praise (from the right person) works. It's why peer pressure usually works. It's why bullying is so demoralizing, debilitating, and detrimental to mental and physical health.

Bullying undermines the message we try to teach others to convey: "I am doing good, so notice me. Emulate me. Carry on my work." Today's corporate behemoths and raiders with questionable practices and politics are undermining that message too. To combat bullying, in particular corporate bullying, I am advocating that we redefine what *outsource* means in entrepreneurship and, frankly, in life.

Big business has a history of using bullying tactics to get ahead. Years ago in school I learned about the concept of a monopoly and studied the Antitrust Law and the 1982 breakup of Ma Bell, the telephone company known for years as the "bully on the block." Today's students will soon discuss today's corporate bullies, such as Apple and Microsoft joining forces against Google, ushering in a period of anti-progress and anti-entrepreneurship. Dan Lyons, one of my go-to thought leaders on tech, wrote about this on 4 November 2013 in his new series of blogposts for Hubspot, *Up and to the Right* (http://bit.ly/apple-microsoft-impede-progress). Lyons, a respected journalist and tech blogger who studies Apple-related business trends, points out that the decision to join forces against Google will not only hurt productivity within Apple and Microsoft but will affect the lives of many other people around the world. Lives of consumers, lives of future students and entrepreneurs, and lives of all those children who could have been helped with money now going for legal fees, investigators, and customs officials.

What a waste. I responded immediately to this spot-on analysis when I saw it on LinkedIn. Here's what I wrote: "In medieval times, 'Right is Might' kept feudalism, actual clan feuds, and archaic thinking alive. Now, while the Digital Age's in full swing, and capitalism and collaborative/social entrepreneurship have gained footholds all over the world, it's interesting and disturbing to see that way of thinking permeating the ongoing Apple vs. Google war. Making for negative, global impacts for the consumer, the marketer, the ed-tech professional/consultant, and students in schools trying to learn and progress. We've just gone backwards, not forwards, in the Tech Revolution!"

I believe that social incentives in business must take into account the long-term effects a transaction has on the supply and demand chain. It must also account for the impact of the conduct of others, learned by example. We need to start thinking about outsourcing our resources instead of mismanaging or hoarding them. This applies to best practices regarding sustainability, as well as philanthropy and economic, educational, and social reform.

Take the new environmental campaign by the Patagonia Company. I'm impressed with the recent post, "The Responsible Economy," by founder Yvon Chouinard (http://bit.ly/responsible-economy). In it he writes, "We are no longer called 'citizens.' Economists, government and Wall Street call us 'consumers.' We 'destroy, waste, squander, use up,' and that's just *Webster's* definition. The sad truth is that the world economy revolves around our consumption."

Chouinard then asks an important question for both the entrepreneur/provider and consumer to ask themselves: "Can we even imagine what an economy would look like that wouldn't destroy the home planet?" This essay clearly proposes environmental reform, which is something that all entrepreneurs have a responsibility to think about when implementing their plan. But you also have a responsibility to think about your actions as harbingers for social reform, which will be studied and emulated by others no matter which industry you target or what product or service you sell.

I want to encourage you to think outside the box about this. I want to propose that you use social incentives to network with others in the short term in order to encourage buyers and consumers of your service or product to keep in touch and come back for an encore performance. Set yourself up as a source, albeit one with a relatively short shelf life.

An entrepreneur can use social incentives as a way to outsource, invoking real change by engaging in both mentorship and reverse mentorship (which I covered in the previous chapter). Outsourcing yourself — your knowledge, skill set, strengths, perspectives, and time — results in long-term benefits. These benefits include an opportunity to intellectually and emotionally grow as an entrepreneur and as a person and, in turn, help others to grow. Being informed is the greatest asset human beings have to expand their milieu and horizons and to counteract inertia. Inertia resulting from outdated viewpoints, stagnant behaviors, and poor time management. These are all potential pitfalls that entrepreneurs encounter in the behaviors of others the more they collaborate to spur change.

So my suggestion to you is to outsource. Be informed. Be a mentor. Be a mentee. Provide *meaningful* content on your social media sites. Volunteer. Stay curious. Be a student of life, for life. Hopefully you'll be around a while and have much to contribute.

I escaped the oppressive afternoon heat of a June day (and rewarded myself for finishing a huge chunk of writing for this book) by stepping into a movie theatre to see *The Internship*. It was billed as a bromance about two old-school salesmen who lose their jobs, forcing them to consider their options. They are ecstatic to get accepted as summer interns at Google in San Francisco. As an Apple techie I was curious to see the inside of Google's "bat cave." Rumor had it that the movie was actually filmed inside Google headquarters. It was. I was curious about the competition and the truth behind the urban legends and rumors.

It was interesting to see elements of the Google ecosystem up close. On many levels. Rumors of bias toward hiring millennials. Rumors about an improved ratio of male/female interns. Rumors of increased attempts to provide a better work/life balance for employees. Some rumors have been laid to rest by this movie. Some were recently laid to rest or added to the list in an article by Matt Asay on 24 October 2013, entitled, "People Buy From Apple But Want to Work for Google, Study Finds" (http://bit.ly/work-for-google). Asay writes that while "critical employees complained about how big the company is, and the difficulty of connecting with other employees or management, apparently these are viewed as lesser evils compared to Apple's tough time demands." It seems that, overall, people are happy working for Google, whose social incentives sparked the antitrust lawsuit about employee poaching.

As an entrepreneur who is curious about patterns and people, I was fascinated by the journey that both 40-something salesmen, who did not appear to have previous work/life balance, job satisfaction, and perhaps even self-respect, took, from thinking like businessmen to thinking like entrepreneurs. I was also curious to see how they would foster change for themselves and the others they interacted with professionally and personally. I was intrigued by the underlying storyline of how social incentive acts as a catalyst for these two men. They pushed themselves in different ways to study and succeed.

Nick, played by Owen Wilson as a goofy, ever-chipper guy, is motivated by his interest in Dana, one of Google's top brass, played winsomely by Rose Byrne. Billy, played poignantly and humorously by Vince Vaughn, is motivated by the faith that Nick and his team of much younger interns place in him during the competitions for a coveted spot in that office, after the internship is over. Billy inadvertently engages in both mentorship and reverse mentorship, ultimately earning him the attention of a high-ranking "Googler." I hate spoilers, so I won't elaborate in case some female readers now change their minds and decide to see this geeky movie. What I learned about entrepreneurship in my own journey can be seen in the movie, too, summarized by three words: persistence, collaboration, and transparency. I recommend this movie for both its educational and entertainment value.

Moral Incentives = Think *Resource.*
Be COMPETENT.

BELIEVE that it's your moral and ethical imperative to leave a legacy behind — a physical legacy (sustainability, philanthropy) and a metaphysical legacy (altruism, mentorship, meaningful content curation). I believe it should be a life-long mission to leave the world and the people in it in better shape than it was when you were born. I wrote about that in the beginning of this book. While I consider faith to be important, a theological treatise is beyond my scope, and certainly not the point of this book. The point of this book is for me to provide a blueprint for female entrepreneurs to orchestrate change — purposeful, innovative, and humane change with far-reaching effects — socially, educationally, technologically, economically, and environmentally.

Your service or product is your currency, and you need to barter it carefully, globally, and creatively as you journey towards your worthy goal. All the while keeping in mind the need to devise and actualize your legacy. Your competence lies in achievement through the use of your internal drive and a moral compass to succeed. I believe it can also be measured in the legacy you leave behind, even while still on this earth, allowing others to benefit from the *resource* your service or product can and will become.

While I'm obviously an advocate of embedding social entrepreneurship into your entrepreneurial DNA, I would like to point out what one of my favorite startup entrepreneur thought leaders writes about it. In his blogpost on 29 August 2013 entitled, "Are You a Social Entrepreneur?" Martin Zwilling defines a social entrepreneur as one who tries "to generate *social value,* rather than profits, and use traditional business principles to create and manage a venture to make social change." He cautions you to remember that "whether the objective is to generate profits or social capital, the common element for all entrepreneurs is the recognition that there is a problem which needs solving, or there is an opportunity to improve the status quo." Zwilling then goes on to list what social entrepreneurship is not. It's worth a read (http://bit.ly/social-entrepreneur), even if you don't feel defined by those parameters.

Whether you're uncomfortable placing yourself in that space, or comfortable pursuing entrepreneurship using different methodologies, I recommend that you keep in mind the point about moral incentives raised by Patrick Hull in his 4 October 2013 article for *Forbes*. It's entitled "Entrepreneurs Should Be Community Leaders" (http://bit.ly/entrepreneurs-should-be-community-leaders). In it he writes that "entrepreneurs, by definition, are leaders. Communities need someone with a vision who can see the potential for improvement in a specific area. We are problem solvers and disruptors; we think creatively; we are resourceful. I think we all have a responsibility to give back to our communities and help others in whatever ways we can." He then gives two ways to become leaders, and writes about the impact community service had on him, others, and his company's networking practices and overall brand.

It's too bad some other companies and business people didn't think like this! In October 2001 the Enron scandal rocked the world. It forever changed the face of Wall Street and subsequently the face of commerce as we know it. To me the executives involved were certainly not motivated by moral incentives. Their greed caused them to bypass morals and go straight for economic incentives, consequences be damned. But humanity, already facing a world of poverty, hunger, depleted resources, and wars without end, can no longer function on the basis of economic incentives alone.

The Freakonomics Duo lists three distinct types of incentive: economic, social, and moral. More people need to consider advocating for moral incentives that come from within, which will then influence their navigation system, their internal GPS, in guiding them when they pursue economic and social incentives. But don't just take my word for it. Read *Smartest Guys in the Room: The Amazing Rise and Scandalous Fall of Enron* by Bethany McLean and Peter Elkind for their take on it.

The Enron executives who were eventually found guilty of skimming money (stealing, fraud, fabricating documents, and other violations) were ridiculed and prosecuted. Their reputations and legacies were destroyed, just as they destroyed so many lives near and far. They attempted to buy themselves financial freedom at the cost of the well-being of others. Their own freedom was later curtailed — they were all jailed. Interestingly, the scandal was revealed a month after the 9/11 terror attack on American soil. Another attempt by short-term thinkers to curtail freedom. Patterns. Seemingly random events but actually part of a pattern.

A successful female entrepreneur understands patterns, exploits them positively, and tries to be a long-term resource for others. Life is about studying patterns around us — in nature, in the actions of others, and in events in our lives — and committing that knowledge of patterns to our minds for future reference (episodic memories). So that we can recall which behaviors to repeat and emulate and which behaviors to discount and discard when faced with similar, new, or repeating situations. So that we can instigate educational, environmental, social, economic, and moral reform based on the lessons we learn and transmit to others.

Successful entrepreneurship is predicated upon both our innate and learned understanding of how the ever-changing world works and how to redefine our fluctuating role in it. How to apply previously learned lessons to future events and patterns that appear before us. How to bridge the past with the present and future in order to understand and redirect those patterns to improve situations for the next generation.

It's in our individual DNA to nurture and be concerned for the well-being of others. It's in our collective DNA to want to leave the world a better place for our children and our children's children. As

I wrote in my preface, we're hard-wired to measure overall job satisfaction and pride in our performance by calibrating how much of a positive impact we have on our community, not just ourselves. So my advice to you is to develop and hone different skills to expand your knowledge base on a variety of topics, build on your own learning style and multiple intelligences, exit your mental, physical, and emotional comfort zones to try new things, enrich your own theory of mind, and unleash your creativity. It will all positively affect your ability to problem solve and connect the dots. I recommend that you create a *convergence of competency,* resulting in behaving in such a way that you're seen as a resource to teach others. To orchestrate positive change in the way others live their lives.

Exchange Your Mantras: Be a Myth-buster. Think *Outside the Box.* Be an ENTREPRENEUR.

GROWING UP with the American Dream right after the era that birthed the women's movement, heralded space travel as a real possibility in the not-so-distant future, and produced the first personal computer, I've seen the power of education, which is the driving force behind any revolution. Education, however, can be wielded as a double-edged sword. Many women in the workforce are still exposed to conflicting messages about their many roles, the moral evils of capitalism and sometimes even technology, and the erosion of the nuclear family. Pervasive myths are passed around as wise sayings. Myths that I believe are self-defeating for female entrepreneurs to say aloud, let alone believe. I can't tell you how many times I've cringed when I heard these three myths directed at me by well-meaning teachers, colleagues, friends, and relatives since I was a little girl:

- ⊛ *You can have it all.*
- ⊛ *Curiosity killed the cat.*
- ⊛ *Wait for the right time.*

Myth #1: You Can Have it All

Life is one big juggling act — intellectual, psychological, and financial. Many balls get juggled in the air, but there's always one ball that you intentionally view close up and have a particular interest in levitating. You divide your attention among your various balls (goals, projects, jobs, etc.), knowing that your focus is on the one. That's the one task that will probably be completed first and best. There's no shame in that — it's a reality of human timing and the way our brains are hard-wired.

When I'm simultaneously attempting to work out on a treadmill, type a report on an iPad, cook a pot of soup, talk on the phone, and mentally write a grocery list, I will get the jobs done. Eventually. But there's a price to be paid for the divided attention. Mental fatigue. Guilt. Perfectionism. Missed opportunities. Lack of gestalt thinking. Disorganization. Unhealthy, unproductive traits for anyone to have, let alone an entrepreneur.

I've learned the hard way, as many will attest, that you can feel like you have it all, but only for a short time. At the end of the day, female entrepreneurs have to ask themselves these questions: Which ball in the air is the real focal point right now? Why? For how long? Then what? That focal point is the one to monitor and concentrate on, even if it means putting the other balls (goals, projects, jobs, etc.) on the periphery, on your back burner. For a while.

When I was 21 I started graduate school at New York University full time while working as a special education teacher. I had a full-time schedule and was feeling added pressure to keep up with friends, grow up fast, and make my parents proud by settling down. Halfway through my first semester, the pressure was getting to me. Not enough sleep and too many demands on my time. Something had to give.

Support came from an unexpected source. My paternal grandmother, whom I adored and who knew me so well (we shared a bedroom all through high school after all), heard me having a minor meltdown and intervened. She stood up for me. Vocally. Quietly but firmly. I never forgot it. My soft-spoken, gentle, immigrant grand-mother said a few deceptively simple words. That's all it took. For me to gain clarity of purpose, focus, and, yes, start to feel good about the choices I made. "You need to make a difference and help people. But first you need time. You deserve time to learn how to stand up on your own two feet before you help others do the same. Life doesn't work out as planned. Look at me, widowed young, with no prospects, left with two young children in a new country. Nobody has it all."

My grandmother understood me and was proud of me. Of my desire for a meaningful career. Of my drive to succeed and help others do the same. Of my deep longing to instigate change. Traits innate and learned — all of which she helped instill in me. My grandmother passed soon after I earned my master's degree in speech-language pathology, but her words have lingered to this day. To show me the path to take, which balls to juggle and focus on, and which myths to ignore.

Women today have many opportunities to juggle priorities, ride the seesaw of multitasking, and contribute a legacy — in different arenas and in different time periods. In *Lean In,* Sheryl Sandberg writes about these opportunities. I recommend it for women everywhere to gain insight into the challenges we're still facing in the present workplace. In the book there's a quote by Tina Fey about the differences between the way men and women think and are perceived in society. According to Fey — trailblazer, writer, actor, mother, and voted by women the all-around best gal pal — one of the worst questions a woman can be asked is, "How do you juggle it all?" Why? Because it's disrespectful. Because it's presumptuous. Because it's uninformed. Asking that question undermines a woman's self-confidence and results in her believing that her efforts are going unnoticed, or worse, they're insufficient.

Many of us have read Fey's hilarious, perceptive, plainspoken observations in her bestseller, *Bossypants.* I recommend it to all female entrepreneurs for both its humor and reflections about humanity. One passage in the book in particular resonated with me. I feel that we women are a different breed from men, male entrepreneurs in particular. That's why I was so taken with Fey's Rules of Improvisation on pages 84–85. Those two pages sum up ways in which women can more successfully contribute to those around them and more successfully navigate the balancing act of life and work. Fey provides keen strategies to implement, whether it be when conversing with others or trying to carve out a place for yourself professionally. Not "having it all" all of the time, but making sure to "have more of it" over time.

Fey brilliantly suggests that to do so women should do more of the following:

1. **Agree.** "Start with a yes and see where that takes you."

2. **Make statements.** "Whatever the problem, be part of the solution. Make statements with your actions and your voice."

3. **Make mistakes.** "There are no mistakes, only opportunities. Many of the world's greatest discoveries have been by accident."

I would suggest to female entrepreneurs: map out your game plan, highlighting your stops along the way and the length of time it will take to achieve your goals. Keep your eyes on the ball. Scaffold your accomplishments. Make and learn from your mistakes. Timing is everything. But you can creatively and cognitively harness time to make it work for you. As Madeleine Albright said, "I do think that women can have it all, just not at the same time."

Understanding this simple truth changes your entire approach. It impacts your decisions regarding your priorities, work/life balance, productivity, and focus; when to engage and disengage from projects, mentors, and clients; and when to live in the moment vs. plan for the future. There's a lot of virtual mentorship and thought leadership on this subject that can help you with your own trajectory .

Here's some additional food for thought:

- ⌁ http://bit.ly/perfect-your-work-life-balance
- ⌁ http://bit.ly/powerful-ways-to-spend-a-day
- ⌁ http://bit.ly/refocus-your-vision
- ⌁ http://bit.ly/your-bodys-best-time-for-everything
- ⌁ http://bit.ly/tips-for-busy-people
- ⌁ http://bit.ly/get-work-flexibility

Myth #2: Curiosity Killed the Cat

I never understood this phrase. First, I'm a big believer in curiosity, in asking "Why not?" I've done so as a child, which earned me many scoldings and many threats of detention in school, or worse, impromptu visits to the principal's office. Asking "Why not?" encourages individuality, creativity, and thinking outside the box. Thanks to Apple and the subsequent inventions by its competitors, the Tech Revolution has brought about a renaissance in cultural and informational consumption. It's resulted in a resurgence of individualization in how we come by that consumption. It's also transformed self-actualization, as we redefine ourselves by the digital avatars and mobile devices that are now extensions of ourselves, pushing the envelope regarding what's impossible.

The rules have changed for the new music of life. Music that has a new refrain: Why not? We're currently living in the "iEra," an age of individualization through tech, where the question "Why not?" has never been more relevant. You need to be a lifelong student of the "Why not?" school of thought to counteract inertia, boredom, and arrogance. Especially now when people are living longer lives in a morally ambiguous and globally connected society.

A curious person is a person who never stops questioning and therefore never stops learning. A curious person wants to understand things — about events and about people. Curiosity facilitates your intellectual and emotional growth because it fosters your theory of mind and emotional attunement — with your environment and those in it.

And I don't know why this phrase has to malign the poor cat! I happen to be severely allergic to cats and nobody's idea of a stereotypical cat person. Yet I would think that this antiquated phrase would be disliked today based on our collective affinity for animals. Look how many pet stores and zoos we have in the United States alone. There's even a book ranking them: *America's Best Zoos* by Allen Nyhuis and Jon Wassner. Look at all the cats living in people's homes. Look at all the Disney movies featuring feline friends. Look at how popular stuffed animals are with babies and toddlers. Why is this phrase still being used?

One of the most profound essays I ever read was "All I Really Need to Know I Learned in Kindergarten," written by Robert Fulghum. I had it framed for my office and have shared it with my seminar audiences for years. It's a testimonial to the social development of a child. It's also a doctrine about learning. In it are wise words to live by. As a human being. As an entrepreneur. Words about the realities of multitasking and the benefits of curiosity. I will only partially quote it, but I strongly suggest that you read it in its entirety.

Live a balanced life — learn some and think some
and draw and paint and sing and dance and play
and work every day some.

When you go out into the world, watch out for traffic,
hold hands, and stick together.

Be aware of wonder.

And then remember the Dick-and-Jane books
and the first word you learned — the biggest
word of all — LOOK.

You need to be curious in order to orchestrate change. A curious person isn't satisfied with the status quo. A curious person knows the importance of education and constant learning to be used as stepping stones to accrue more knowledge. A curious person studies patterns and alters his or her own behavior accordingly, based on the new information provided. Isn't that what entrepreneurship is all about?

Here's some additional food for thought:

- http://bit.ly/how-to-develop-curiosity
- http://bit.ly/standing-in-curiosity
- http://bit.ly/how-curiosity-fosters-change
- http://bit.ly/energizing-curiosity

Myth #3: Wait for the Right Time

Because of biological and cultural factors, women, more so than men, are more sensitive to the rhythms of time. They are more sensitive despite technological advances, medical advances, and the feminist movement. I'm not trying to derail the feminist movement or instigate a furious debate. I'm trying to point out that a woman's innate sensitivity to time makes the way she multitasks, approaches problems, and strives to accomplish tasks different from the way a man does these things.

On one hand, we women want to forge ahead and fulfill our own manifest destiny — even if it's initially all in our head, even if we end up starting small. On the other hand, because of our historically and biologically inculcated aversion to risk, female entrepreneurship has been lagging, especially in the STEM (science, technology, engineering, math) arenas.

We all know and understand that timing is everything. I previously wrote about the concept of cognitive timing and how channeling it deliberately can provide you with the momentum needed to shift focus, break patterns, and propel you to change behavior. I also wrote about certain prerequisite skills entrepreneurs need to have and the steps they need to take to hone them. Specific readiness indicators leading up to that epiphany, that eureka moment, that all entrepreneurs need in order to engage. At the same time, as an entrepreneur you need to trust your instinct and take the plunge, or just do it, as the Nike commercials tell us. An entrepreneur needs to redirect time and understand how to make it work for her.

Understanding the importance of timing is why I recommend *Time Warped* in my entrepreneurial reading list, despite it not being a typical business book. In it psychology writer and BBC broadcaster Claudia Hammond writes about the neuropsychological theories and research behind individuals' stories and new findings about the elasticity of time. She writes about the human perception of time passing, the ability to shape it, and even includes an entire chapter on how you can change your relationship with time and make it work for you. Hammond provides one example after another that "illustrates the central theme of this book — that we are creating our own perceptions of time, based on the neuronal activity in our brains with input from the physiological symptoms of our bodies." Hammond's futuristic title evokes images of that elusive starship Enterprise from Gene Roddenberry's *Star Trek* universe, which may give you pause. In reality, the book is a very interesting, easy-to-read, relevant, and surprisingly user-friendly manual. It's filled with practical time-management tips, applicable to people everywhere, especially entrepreneurs. "Time can be a friend, but it can also be an enemy. The trick is to harness it, whether at home, at work, or even in social policy, and to work in line with our conception of time. Time perception matters because it is the experience of time that roots us in our mental reality. Time is not only at the heart of the way we organize life, but the way we experience it."

A cell phone commercial hit the airwaves. It's a really funny one. Virgin Mobile has created a catchphrase, a mantra, that's so apropos to the point I'm making. The mantra is "It's Time to Retrain Your Brain." The ad is already on YouTube (http://bit.ly/retrain-your-brain-commercial), and I encourage you to see it for yourself. Why? Because the visual imagery, albeit with subliminal messages for marketing purposes, hits home a crucial point. The images of the cup with the overflowing coffee, as well as the woman in a hot tub filled with cash, provide the message I'm trying to get across here. The truth about time.

Efficient time management and methodical planning for the future entail the cognitive restructuring of time in your mind. Part of that is doing a mental cost analysis of your return for having spent that time on that endeavor. Best practices in marketing include understanding the return on investment (ROI). That involves understanding the trade-off between the time and effort you put into your service or product and what you get out of it.

So waiting for the right time is actually detrimental to accurately reshaping and planning your schedule and to-do lists. You need to adopt more proactive strategies about time management instead of reacting to it from a crisis intervention paradigm. You need to stop being passive in the face of passing moments. You need to dial down or better channel your self-protective instinct to avoid risk and wait and see.

In *The Art of the Start* Guy Kawasaki writes about cognitively retraining your brain's self-protective instinct to wait and see. The book provides a terrific road map for entrepreneurs wanting to know about the lay of the land, from branding to bootstrapping and everything in between. I highly recommend it. Dr. Spencer Johnson writes more about the adaptive nature of time and the pitfalls of a wait-and-see attitude in *Who Moved My Cheese?* It's a short, funny, insightful parable about how to address your fear of risk, fear of change, and fear of failure. I suggest his book too.

We're living in increasingly uncertain and complex times. That's why entrepreneurs need to use time, not let it use them. As entrepreneur Jim Rohn said, "Either you run the day or the day runs you." Seth Godin writes in *Linchpin*, "It's impossible to follow the manual because there is no manual." Godin succinctly argues my point about debunking the myth of waiting for the right time in his thought-provoking, methodically written book. Godin writes, "That is why linchpins are so valuable during times of great complexity (which is most of the time). Linchpins make their own maps and thus allow the organization to navigate more quickly than it ever could if it had to wait for the paralyzed crowd to figure out what to do next."

Wise words. Timely words. No pun intended. Learn to become a linchpin. We women need you. The world needs you. As I just wrote, timing is everything. You can creatively and cognitively harness it to make it work for you. So that you can then make it work for others. I created The NICE Initiative and launched it with the hope that we can all work together. To provide each other with strategies, forums, seminars, and opportunities to help more women partake of both the Entrepreneurial and Tech Revolutions, which have now intersected. It's time. Start now.

Here's some additional food for thought:

- http://bit.ly/find-flow-in-your-work
- http://bit.ly/sustainable-business-requires-time
- http://bit.ly/become-an-expert-in-an-hour
- http://bit.ly/be-productive-not-busy
- http://bit.ly/habits-of-effective-mediocre-people
- http://bit.ly/importance-of-mindfulness

Conclusion

KEY WEBSITES

- ✐ http://bit.ly/your-digital-to-do-list
- ✐ http://bit.ly/advice-for-solopreneurs
- ✐ http://bit.ly/its-ok-if-your-startup-isnt-changing-the-world-yet
- ✐ http://bit.ly/why-planning-is-ruining-your-business
- ✐ http://bit.ly/you-dont-need-to-be-all-powerful
- ✐ http://bit.ly/thought-leadership-is-change-leadership

Quotes to Ponder

Do the things you know and you shall learn the truth you need to know.

— Louisa May Alcott

Every child is an artist. The problem is how to remain one when we grow up.

— Pablo Picasso

HAVE YOU EVER seen children at play? Over my years as a sibling, babysitter, teacher, speech therapist, and aunt, I've seen many. During my many conversations with both parents and professionals in my field, on the home front and at my seminars, I have discussed children's behavior, interests, thematic play schemas, and reactions to their environment, and the time constraints placed upon them in their environment. I've seen children admonished by the phrase, "wait for the right time," but *they often don't listen!*

How many adults jump right into a pool instead of dipping in a toe? How many children do a cannonball or running leap right into the water? How many adults wait to cry in private, where nobody can see, because they perceive tears as a sign of weakness? How many children tear up and release the waterworks on the playground one minute and are happily chattering the next? To the

same child who made them cry in the first place? This leads me to my final list of pointers seen through a unique lens, through the eyes of a child. Here's what I've learned and want to share, hoping that it will help you too.

Penina's Pointers

What Children Can Teach NICE Entrepreneurs

1. **Be emotionally open.** Be prepared to show kindness, honest passion, and vulnerability. Emote. Be emotionally engaged with others. Embrace your own feelings and mistakes. Forgive and forget how the feelings and mistakes of others affected you.

2. **Be curious.** Invest in a current library card and/or technology (classes, webinars, demos, etc.) to keep learning. Visit an Apple Store. Take in a workshop or attend a conference, or try an online course. Check out Coursera.org. Check out a TED talk. Check out *The Huffington Post*'s many sections and articles. Read! Books. Blogs. Fiction. Nonfiction. See what headlines are appearing on sites like Alltop, Slate, Digg, and in

your Zite app. Explore the outdoors. Converse with strangers. Travel — near and far. Become adaptable.

3. **Be industrious.** Develop hobbies and skills. Try to expand them and apply what you've learned to other situations. Work hard. Play harder. Find a balance that works for you. Become better able to self-regulate, and engage in more productive time-management behaviors. Have to-do lists and break them down. Make multiple ones. Learn to view technology as your ally, your virtual assistant, and your friend.

4. **Be honest.** With yourself. With others. Ask for feedback. Provide accurate feedback. Politely. Humbly. Effectively. Humorously. Be yourself, and stay true to yourself.

5. **Be optimistic.** Approach each new day and opportunity with enthusiasm, self-confidence, and humor, especially on those hard days. Be cheerful about the small things. Be resilient and stoic (after having a good cry) about the large things. Change the way you view obstacles, setbacks, and the unknown. Be in touch with your "inner child" who sees the wonder all around. Let yourself suspend disbelief and feel awe. Let yourself engage in "self-talk" and wishful thinking and daydreaming.

6. **Be present.** Live in the moment. Don't dwell on the past or fret about the future. Enjoy what you have and what you are doing at this moment in time. Embrace the now. With all you've got. Develop better powers of observation and deep listening. Increase

> your attention and decrease your multitasking and compartmentalizations.
>
> 7. **Be eager.** To tell and hear stories. Use your listening skills. Discern patterns. Identify the various elements of the story arc and what you learned from each one. Hone your creativity, imagination, and flair for drama when retelling them. Pay attention. Ask questions. Make time for stories again.

There you have it. My final round of Penina's Pointers for female entrepreneurs, newly minted or seasoned, stateside or worldwide, based upon my NICE philosophy. I write about what I know. I know a bit about child development. I also took the advice of Austin Kleon, author of the creative *Steal Like An Artist,* who recommends that you should write the book you want to read. I wanted to learn how to positively exploit economic, cultural, and technological patterns to spur change. I wanted to view entrepreneurship through the innately honest, simplified lens of a child. Talk about reverse mentorship! Talk about developing and analyzing patterns! You can learn so much from a child. I have. You have. We can all do so again. I've provided the information. The rest is up to you. As one of my early mentors, Dr. Susan Fralick-Ball, PsyD, MSN, says, "The journey *is* the blessing!" We are all works in progress. I for one hope to remain so. I wish you all much luck, success, progress, and enlightening and rewarding travels. Enjoy the ride!

APPENDIX A

Online Resources for Entrepreneurs

Quotes to Ponder

In life, all good things come hard, but wisdom is the hardest to come by.

— Lucille Ball

You can get help from teachers, but you are going to have to learn a lot by yourself, sitting alone in a room.

— Theodore Geisel (Dr. Seuss)

I WROTE BEFORE that the spirit of the Wild West seems to be alive and well in the iOS App Store. I would like to say the same for website traffic regarding all things entrepreneurial. From well-known business magazine hubs to obscure blogs, from social media sites to millennial generation portals, it's all here, waiting for you to find. I try to keep up as best I can, using Safari's Reading List and my iOS Zite app in conjunction with both my Evernote and Pocket apps to save curated content that I can learn from and share with others. I also peruse Alltop.com, Slate.com, and Digg.com and use the iOS app Newsify and the Feedly Reader, which is connected to my Google+ account to stay current. In addition, I peruse two websites in particular once or twice a month that help me get a visual snap-shot of websites I'm interested in: StumbleUpon and Pearltrees. In a nutshell this has become my overall workflow that enables me to become a bona fide entrepreneur.

Since I began writing this book it's occurred to me that female entrepreneurship, like anything else, involves homework, practice, choices, and opportunities. I therefore went into my Safari book-marks, synced across all my Apple devices in iCloud, and cross-referenced them with my content from my other digital portfolios, which I just listed above. I analyzed the data and realized that a pat-tern emerged. A pattern showing my tendency to gravitate toward succinct, visually rich, content-rich, multidisciplinary, and multi-cultural websites that feature entrepreneurial resources and recipes for integration with technology, best practices, and social media. I therefore decided to list only those sites that fit the bill. Here are helpful links to help you learn more about the nuts and bolts of entrepreneurship, in keeping with the themes of this book. These sites are constantly updated, and new ones appear regularly. Stay vigilant and create your own digital portfolio so you can share your lists with others. I wouldn't mind having you share them with me by e-mailing me at penina@niceinitiative.com. I'll give you the credit when I post them.

Thirty Links for NICE Entrepreneurs

- http://bit.ly/sba-office-of-womens-business-ownership
- http://bit.ly/women-in-stem
- http://bit.ly/lean-in-womens-community
- http://bit.ly/project-eve-inspiring-women
- http://bit.ly/ms-magazine
- http://bit.ly/pam-slim-blog
- http://bit.ly/slate-magazine
- http://bit.ly/digg-top-stories
- http://bit.ly/morguefile-free-photos
- http://bit.ly/wall-street-journal-online
- http://bit.ly/entrepreneur-magazine
- http://bit.ly/entrepreneur-magazine-women
- http://bit.ly/forbes-magazine
- http://bit.ly/inc-magazine
- http://bit.ly/business-insider-magazine
- http://bit.ly/small-business-trends
- http://bit.ly/the-jane-dough-for-career-women
- http://bit.ly/freakonomics online
- http://bit.ly/young-entrepreneur-magazine
- http://bit.ly/social-media-examiner
- http://bit.ly/savvy-chick-tech-news
- http://bit.ly/chick-ceo
- http://bit.ly/young-fabulous-self-employed-magazine
- http://bit.ly/under-30-ceo
- http://www.kickstarter.com
- http://bit.ly/seth-godin-blog
- http://bit.ly/alltop-headline-aggregator
- http://bit.ly/slideshare-presentation-aggregator
- http://bit.ly/pearltrees-information-organizer
- http://bit.ly/stumbleupon-web-page-discovery

Twenty Links for Balancing Cravings for Humanity and Technology

- http://bit.ly/tech-influence-over-humanity
- http://bit.ly/questions-to-ask-before-posting
- http://bit.ly/value-of-social-media
- http://bit.ly/drucker-on-entrepreneurship
- http://bit.ly/what-colors-communicate
- http://bit.ly/relationships-matter
- http://bit.ly/unleash-your-inner-artist
- http://bit.ly/social-media-influencers
- http://bit.ly/how-to-be-a-better-person
- http://bit.ly/written-words-and-the-future
- http://bit.ly/enhancing-creativity
- http://bit.ly/social-media-obsession
- http://bit.ly/huff-post-redefining-success
- http://bit.ly/leadership-matters
- http://bit.ly/valeria-maltoni-blog
- http://bit.ly/denise-brosseau-blog
- http://bit.ly/mark-crowley-lead-from-the-heart
- http://bit.ly/bruce-kasanoff
- http://bit.ly/jay-deragon-relationship-economy-blog
- http://bit.ly/brian-solis-blog

Fifteen Links for Increasing Your Content Marketing and Overall Social Media Marketing Savvy

- http://bit.ly/hootsuite-social-media-management
- http://bit.ly/michelle-killebrew-blog
- http://bit.ly/reekah-radice-blog
- http://bit.ly/dangers-of-inconsistent-branding
- http://bit.ly/content-marketing-strategies
- http://bit.ly/why-you-need-content-marketing
- http://bit.ly/use-slideshare-to-grow-your-business
- http://bit.ly/social-media-design-tips
- http://bit.ly/choosing-a-social-media-platform
- http://bit.ly/how-blogging-helps-you-dominate-search
- http://bit.ly/google-plus-posting-guide
- http://bit.ly/content-marketing-vs-social-media
- http://bit.ly/tips-to-grow-your-email-list
- http://bit.ly/social-media-predictions-for-2014
- http://bit.ly/curate-content-or-create-it

APPENDIX B

Reading List for Entrepreneurs

Quotes to Ponder

Never go to a doctor whose office plants have died.

— Erma Bombeck

If women are expected to do the same work as men, we must teach them the same things.

— Plato

THERE ARE COUNTLESS BOOKS out there on various aspects of business and entrepreneurship. Some are dry tomes written by experts on economic theory. Some are technical manuals written by bottom-line-thinking, corporate CEOs. Some are easy to understand, others are hard to get through. Many cover financial aspects of self-employment while others cover ways to assemble an entrepreneurial dream team. There aren't, however, many books on entrepreneurship by women, and I really tried to find them. I spent time in my library, in bookstores, online, and in people's homes, perusing bookshelves and taking notes. Some books were helpful, no matter who wrote them, while others were either too esoteric or already obsolete for today's best practices.

Since I formed my own company in 2010, and as I've continued trying to further its growth, I've made repeated attempts to apply my minimalist-behaviorist lens to my self-education. I've since realized that I'm drawn to books that offer stories and practical, easy-to-understand advice and strategies and books that try to answer some of the intellectual and psychological questions about balancing humanity and technology in today's startup culture. That's been my ongoing quest. That's been my point of reference for choosing the books I chose, for myself and for the reading list below.

The books I recommend below are books that have helped me on my ongoing, entrepreneurial journey in various, sometimes circuitous, ways. More importantly, the books listed below have resonated with my theory of mind, which I dubbed the NICE Philosophy when I started to write this book.

I therefore invite you to consider my selected bibliography as just that — considerations for furthering your own theory of mind and philosophies about entrepreneurship. It's obviously not a final list, and I wouldn't want it to be. As I mentioned before, we're all works in progress, and I, for one, secretly hope to remain one in order to forestall stagnant behavior, outdated thinking, and ennui.

Seventy Books for NICE Entrepreneurs

Acuff, John (2013). *Start: Punch Fear in the Face, Escape Average, and Do Work That Matters.* Nashville, Tennessee: Thomas Nelson.

Allen, David (2001). *Getting Things Done.* New York: Penguin Group.

Anderson, Chris (2008). *The Long Tail.* New York: Hyperion.

Arison, Sherry (2013). *Activate Your Goodness.* New York: Hay House.

Belsky, Scott (2010). *Making Ideas Happen.* New York: Penguin Group.

Bernoff, Josh, and Ted Schadler (2010). *Empowered.* Boston: Harvard Business Review Press.

Bhargava, Rohit (2008). *Personality Not Included.* New York: McGraw-Hill.

Blanchard, Ken, Don Hutson, and Ethan Willis (2008). *The One Minute Entrepreneur.* New York: Doubleday.

Blanchard Ken, John Britt, Judd Hoekstra, and Pat Zigarmi (2009). *Who Killed Change?* New York: William Morrow Publishers.

Blank, Steven Gary (2005). *The Four Steps to the Epiphany.* Menlo Park, California: K&S Ranch Consulting.

Bramson, Robert (1981). *Coping With Difficult People.* New York: Dell Publishing.

Burg, Bob, and John David (2007). *The Go Giver.* New York: Penguin Group.

Carnegie, Dale (2009). *How to Win Friends and Influence People.* New York: Simon and Schuster.

Christenson, Clayton (1997). *The Innovator's Dilemma.* Boston: Harvard Business School Press.

Christenson, Clayton. (2003). *The Innovator's Solution.* Boston: Harvard Business School Publishing.

Collins, Jim (2001). *Good to Great.* New York: Harper Collins Publishers.

Covey, Stephen (1989). *The Seven Habits of Highly Effective People.* New York: Fireside.

Covey, Stephen (2008). *The Speed of Trust.* New York: Free Press.

De Bono, Edward (1985). *Six Thinking Hats.* Boston: Little, Brown and Company.

DeLong, David (2004). *Lost Knowledge: Confronting the Threat of an Aging Workforce.* New York: Oxford University Press.

Drucker, Peter (1985). *Innovation and Entrepreneurship.* New York: Harper and Row Publishers.

Duhigg, Charles (2012). *The Power of Habit.* New York: Random House.

Ferrazi, Keith (2005). *Never Eat Alone.* New York: Doubleday.

Ferriss, Timothy (2007). *The 4-Hour Work Week.* New York: Crown Publishing Group.

Fey, Tina (2011). *Bossypants.* New York: Hatchette Book Group.

Fried, Jason, and David Heinemeier Hanson (2010). *Rework.* New York: Crown Publishing Group.

Gerber, Michael (2001). *The E-Myth Revisited.* New York: Harper Collins Publishers.

Gerber, Michael (2009). *The E-Myth Enterprise.* New York: Harper Collins Publishers.

Giesler, Jill (2012). *Work Happy: What Great Bosses Know.* New York: Hatchette Book Group.

Gino, Francesca (2013). *Sidetracked: Why Our Decisions Get Derailed, and How to Stick to the Plan.* Boston: Harvard Business Review Press.

Gladwell, Malcolm (2000). *The Tipping Point: How Little Things Can Make a Big Difference.* New York: Little, Brown, and Company.

Glass, Lillian (1995). *Toxic People.* New York: St. Martin's Griffin.

Godin, Seth (1998). *The Bootstrapper's Bible.* Chicago: Upstart Publishing Company.

Godin, Seth (2008). *Tribes: We Need You to Lead Us.* New York: Penguin Group.

Godin, Seth (2010). *Linchpin: Are You Indispensable?* New York: Penguin Group.

Goldfayn, Alex (2011). *Evangelist Marketing.* Dallas: BenBella Books.

Guillebeau, Cris (2012). *The $100 StartUp.* New York: Crown Business.

Gurian, Michael, and Barbara Annis (2008). *Leadership and the Sexes*. San Francisco: Jossey-Bass.

Halligan, Brian, and Dharmesh Shah (2010). *Inbound Marketing*. Hoboken, NJ: John Wiley & Sons.

Hammond, Claudia (2013). *Time Warped: Unlocking the Mysteries of Time*. New York: Harper Perennial.

Heath, Chip, and Dan Heath (2007). *Made to Stick*. New York: Random House.

Hsieh, Tony (2010). *Delivering Happiness*. New York: Hatchette Book Group.

Isaacson, Walter (2011). *Steve Jobs*. New York: Simon and Schuster.

Jantsch, John (2011). *Duct Tape Marketing Revised and Updated: The World's Most Practical Small Business Marketing Guide*. Nashville: Nelson Business.

Johnson, Spencer (1988). *Who Moved My Cheese?* New York: G. P. Putnam's Sons.

Kawasaki, Guy (1991). *Selling the Dream*. New York: Harper Collins Publishers.

Kawasaki, Guy (2004). *The Art of the Start*. New York: Penguin Books.

Keeley, Larry, Helen Walters, Ryan Pikkel, and Brian Quinn (2013). *Ten Types of Innovation. The Discipline of Building Breakthroughs*. Hoboken, NJ: John Wiley & Sons.

Kim, W. Chan, and Renee Mauborgne (2005). *Blue Ocean Strategy*. Boston: Harvard Business School Publishing.

Kleon, Austin (2012). *Steal Like an Artist*. New York: Workman Publishing Company.

Lafley, A. G., and Roger L. Martin (2013). *Playing to Win*. Boston: Harvard Business School Publishing.

Levin, Martin (2011). *All I Know About Management I Learned from My Dog*. New York: Skyhorse Publishing.

Levinson, Jay Conrad (2007). *Guerrilla Marketing.* Boston: Houghton Mifflin Company.

Levitt, Steven, and Stephen Dubner (2006). *Freakonomics.* New York: Harper Collins Publishers.

Lichtenberg, Ronna (2005). *Pitch Like a Girl: Get Respect. Get Noticed. Get What You Want.* Emmaus, PA: Rodale Books.

Livingston, Jessica (2007). *Founders at Work.* New York: Springer Verlag New York.

Masterson, Michael (2008). *Ready, Fire, Aim.* Hoboken, NJ: John Wiley & Sons.

McCormack, Mark (1984). *What They Don't Teach You At Harvard Business School.* New York: Bantam Books.

Orman, Suze (2007). *Women and Money.* New York: Spiegel and Grau.

Osterwalder, Alexander (2010). *Business Model Generation.* Hoboken, NJ: John Wiley & Sons.

Piasecki, Bruce (2007). *The Surprising Solution: Creating Possibility in a Swift and Severe World.* Naperville, IL: Sourcebooks.

Reis, Eric (2011). *The Lean Startup: How Today's Entrepreneurs Use Continuous Innovation to Create Radically Successful Businesses.* New York: Crown Publishing Group.

Sanberg, Sheryl (2013). *Lean In.* New York: Alfred A. Knopf.

Seidman, Dov. (2011). *How: Why How We Do Anything Means Everything.* Hoboken, NJ: John Wiley & Sons.

Semler, Ricardo. (1993). *Maverick.* New York: Warner Books.

Sinek, Simon (2009). *Start With Why.* New York: Penguin Group.

Slim, Pamela (2009). *Escape from Cubicle Nation.* New York: Penguin Group.

Spence, Roy and Haley Rushing (2009). *It's Not What You Sell, It's What You Stand For.* New York: Penguin Group.

Vaynerchuk, Gary (2009). *Crush It*. New York: Harper Collins Publishers.

Wheeler, Tom (1999). *Leadership Lessons from the Civil War*. New York: Doubleday.

Addendum

You can find more books on balancing cravings for humanity and technology listed on my continually updated Female Entrepreneur Reading List on Amazon Collections:

   ⌐🖰 http://bit.ly/NICE-Reboot-additional-reading

INDEX

ABOUT THE AUTHOR

Penina Rybak is the CEO of Socially Speaking™ LLC, a boutique educational technology consulting firm. In addition to being a startup entrepreneur, Penina is a licensed and practicing pediatric speech-language pathologist specializing in the treatment of autism and an Apple technology expert and iPad evangelist. She lectures nationally and internationally about customizing social communication strategies, integrating iOS apps into best practices in the workplace and in special education settings, and, most recently, on the topic of female entrepreneurship.

Penina has earned an MA from New York University, a Certificate of Clinical Competence for Speech-Language Pathologists from ASHA and is a licensed and certified Teacher of the Speech and Hearing Handicapped. She is also the director of The NICE Initiative for Female Entrepreneurship, whose mission is to promote women founders and startup endeavors and bridge the gap between readiness to learn and actual performance. Over the past three years, Penina has deployed her Socially Speaking™ Social Skills Curriculum, Seminars, and iPad App, as well as her NICE Initiative Seminars.

Penina Rybak MA/CCC-SLP, TSHH

- **CEO:** Socially Speaking™ LLC
- **Director:** The NICE Initiative for Female Entrepreneurship
- **LinkedIn Page:** Penina Rybak http://www.linkedin.com/pub/penina-rybak/37/900/191
- **Email:** penina@niceinitiative.com

- **Website:** http://niceinitiative.com

- **About.Me:** http://about.me/NICE.Initiative/#

- **Twitter:** @PopGoesPenina

- **Tumblr:** The NICE Initiative http://niceinitiative.tumblr.com

- **WordPress Blog for Book:** http://niceinitiativeblog.wordpress.com

- **Pinterest:** Peninaslp http://pinterest.com/peninaslp/the-nice-initiative-for-female-entrepreneurship-tb/

- **Facebook:** The NICE Initiative https://www.facebook.com/TheNiceInitiativeForFemaleEntrepreneurship

- **Google+:** The NICE Initiative http://google.com/+TheNICEInitiativeFemaleEntrepreneurship

- **YouTube:** https://www.youtube.com/user/storytellergal

- **Vimeo:** https://vimeo.com/user19684006

- **Phone:** (646) 820-5547